Social Media Anxiety and Addiction: Breaking Free from the Trap and Taking Back Your Life! Detox Your Brain!

Low Self-Esteem and Negative Effects to Your Health and Relationships

Christopher B. House

Table of Contents

Chapter 1:

Introduction

"Social media has created jealous behavior over illusions. Sadly some are
envious of things, relationships, and lifestyles thatdon't even exist" -
Anonymous

Who would have thought that an idea created by the University
of Pennsylvania graduate, Andrew Weinreich, would be the first
notable form of social media? Before there was Facebook, and
before there was Twitter, Instagram, and Snapchat, there was
SixDegrees.com. This social media platform would lead the
foundation of many forms of networking and connectingtoday.

Though SixDegrees.com lasted from 1997 to 2001, it would give
rise to other more successful and notable platforms that have
become synonymous with the term social media.

The Evolution of SixDegrees to Social Media Giants

For many, if you ask them what social media is, they would not
necessarily be able to describe it, but instead, they would be able
to give you examples of what social media is. According to Tufts
University, social media is best defined as an interactive,
computer, or web-based application that allows the users to share,
create, and engage through information.

When SixDegrees.com first came out, there were over 3 million
users with just under 100 staff members. Though the platform

would be sold to another social media platform, its membership numbers would not come quite as close to what Facebook has in terms of users. As of 2020, Facebook released that there are presently over 2.7 billion active users on their platform.

However, something to note with Facebook is that Facebook is not just a social media platform, but it is also a social media powerhouse. The social media platform was created in 2004 and has since gone on to be worth 524 billion dollars (Kitterman, 2018). This wealth, however, comes from Facebook acquiring other social media platforms. Platforms that Facebook has gone on to acquire include Instagram, WhatsApp, and Friend.ly, to name a few. These acquisitions of anything remotely close to social media have resulted in the rise of Facebook, and what has resulted in many today knowing social media to equate to Facebook.

The Introduction and Uptake of Social Media

How many social media accounts do you have?

Did you know that, according to Omnicore (Kitterman, 2018), a top leading Digital Marketing Agency, the average person has at least eight different social media accounts and will spend a total of two and a half hours a day between their accounts? Remember, social media is defined as any computer or web-based application that allows its users to create and share content.

The eight commonly used social media accounts that individuals have are:

- Facebook
- Youtube
- WhatsApp

- Instagram
- Twitter
- Reddit
- Snapchat
- TikTok

What leads to the rise of these social media platforms? Celebrities and influencers are the most giant propellers of many of these platforms' success and uptake, especially those that came after Facebook and Twitter. These are considered to be the original forms of social media.

For example, TikTok, a social media platform that was created in 2016, has since propelled to be a fast-growing and popular avenue for unique and engaging content. From celebrities to influencers, even politicians from the US and Canada are turning to the platform as a form of engagement with the public.

Why Is Social Media Popular?

For many who struggle to meet people in real life or are interested in meeting new and like-minded individuals, social media allows them to shine and prosper. For example, Pinterest, this social media platform, will enable individuals to share and showcase their cooking, knitting, painting, virtually any talent of theirs, and inspire others to do the same. Pinterest became so prevalent for this that it spawned the hashtag, #PinterestFails.

As a result of the ability to share and showcase one's passions and hobbies, social media has become increasingly popular amongst its users.

Another platform that encourages its users to share and be creative is TikTok. This video clip sharing based platform enables users to lip sync to songs or recreate scenes from their favorite shows and movies. However, what really spiked the interest in

TikTok is the endorsements by celebrities who have gone on these platforms. By being members of these social media platforms, celebrities give their fans a look into their glamorous lifestyle.

Did you know that celebrities who use specific social media platforms drive and increase their interest by ordinary people resulting in an upsurge of new members? Look at the Kardashians; they are notably one of the most famous families who are very active on social media. The Kardashians are known for using social media to release products, to promote their shows and brands; however, there is a dark side to social media...

The Mental Shift Due to Social Media

In 1991, the internet became widely accessible. From there, it snowballed into households across America and, really, the world having access to this new technology. This meant that ordinary and everyday people could, from their home's comforts and within their fingertips, access information that previously would have been accessed from a book. Libraries went from housing encyclopedias and reference books to now housing computers for those unable to afford the at-home internet luxuries (Leiner et al., 2017).

From the internet's creation, the worldwide web became more than just a portal of information and resources; it had suddenly evolved into becoming a social and interactive realm.

Suddenly, users found themselves attracted and addicted to the compliments, the admiration, and the attraction that their online presence was getting. Platforms such as MySpace, HotOrNot, ChatRoulette entered the world wide web and gave people a chance to escape and explore a world beyond their own.

The downfall?

While these early social media platforms' presence gave positive reinforcement, there is a downside for every upside. Unfortunately, social media's constant and quick evolution has resulted in negative and sometimes dire mental health problems. Therapists and health professionals have since then looked at the impacts social media has on one's mental health, including anxiety and self-esteem. The research in this field is just the beginning, as there is also research being done on examining the psychological, linguistic, and emotional development of the users. Given that many are starting to use smart devices as young as five-years-old, there is longitudinal research being done to see what exposure to social media at a young age has on the user.

Some of the earliest research on the psychological and mental impact of social media has shown that users who exhibit addictive and uncontrollable tendencies are at a higher risk of developing, if not exhibiting, anxiety and depression traits. Since this startling and shocking discovery, medical and health professionals are looking at ways of helping teens and youth. Young adults also must learn to overcome the negative and often debilitating effects of social media (Rudin, 2010).

One Day at a Time Learning Process

In this self-help and guided book, I hope to show you the various ways that you can overcome the control that social media has on your life, both emotionally and psychologically.

Will this be an easy process?

No, some days are easier than others, while other days, it will be difficult and hard to break free; however, learning about the lasting impact can help begin the process of weaning off social media and rejoining the simple pleasures of life. Remember, there was a time when we were free from our smart devices and from the constant monitoring of our social media platforms, which means we can attain this lifestyle again.

As you read through this book, I hope that readers will remember that we would never let anyone control our lives, and yet, we allow our smart devices and the social media platforms that were created to keep us connected with loved ones to now hold us back and turn us into prisoners. There is a reason for those sayings of "stop and smell the roses" and "enjoy the small things in life" because it's true. It is important that we take the time to stop and connect with real people, that we connect with those around us and not those we don't see.

Begin the journey and break free from social media's idealized expectations and start a detox to bring you back to YOU!

Chapter 2:

Social Media - What's the Draw?

The Attraction?

"Make sure you are happy in real life not just in social media" -
Anonymous

Do you remember when you passed around notes in class asking
if your crush liked you or not?

Do you remember voting for the most and least popular person
in your grad year?

Social media has taken what we once did on paper and published
in yearbooks and taken it online. Now, there are platforms such
as Facebook, Instagram, TikTok, and Snapchat that allow people
to upload their best looking photo, their memorable experience,
and share it with others in hopes of garnering attention.

This attention is the positive reinforcement that has led to both
mental and self-esteem issues; however, I will delve into this later.

This positive reinforcement is what draws people to these social
media platforms. There is this gratification that not only comes in
the masses but from people they may have never received
recognition from before. This appeal and compliments from
strangers can make someone who has low self-esteem feel
appreciated and wanted. In a way this psychological and mental
impact that social media had on people is what grew the interest
in platforms such as Facebook, Instagram, and Snapchat, to name
a few.

These platforms allow users to upload and share photos of themselves, of their life and in return, people can comment and like it. These small acts of someone hitting "like" and you receiving a "like" can unleash the very same endorphins we get when we are loved and happy. These happy hormones are known to lead and encourage addictions, which is why much of the research on social media often correlates to these life experiences and moments.

One shouldn't feel as though they need to immediately deactivate their accounts. In this chapter, I share the positive and sometimes overlooked side of social media. There is some good that social media brings to the world, and it is important that they be recognized. Why does the positive impact of social media matter? Looking at both sides of the beast which is social media means we can get a better understanding of how it impacts us as a whole.

Why do we get mad when someone disagrees with us?

Why do we get happy when people like what we have to say?

These are questions that this chapter touches on but that this book as a whole covers.

Why Do We CRAVE the Attention of Social Media?

How do you feel when your crush walks by you?

What crosses your mind everytime you bake something and bring it into work?

What is your reaction to the compliments you get after a haircut?

There is a great chance that with any of these scenarios you wanted to feel the same feeling over and over again. When your crush walks by, you are probably wondering, what can I do to get them to walk by me again? When your friends, family, or colleagues compliment your baking, you are probably motivated to bake more. And, when you walk into a room and everyone admires your look, you are determined to always look your best.

These real-life scenarios are exactly what social media does to our minds. The positive reactions we receive propel us to want to desire that feeling over and over again. While at times it may seem that people spend more time online than offline, the reality is that THIS is just how much our lives are so immersed with social media. How we are in face-to-face relationships is sometimes heavily influenced if not motivated by how we are online. On the flip side, however, sometimes, how we portray ourselves online is a false indicator of who we are in person.

For example, if we look at online dating, this is a phenomenon that has spawned applications such as Bumble, Tinder, and OKCupid. These platforms allow people to share their likes and dislikes, while also describing themselves to a potential partner, in hopes of drawing their attention.

Now, chances are you aren't simply going to decide whether or not to marry the person based on an online profile, though it will be the first step in deciding whether or not there is a chance of compatibility; and, hence, meeting them in person. For many people, they believe that the person they chat with online will be the same easy to talk to person in real-life; however, much of the time, this is not the case. In many cases, the person online is confident, sauve, and easy going, while the person in real life is shy, stutters over their words, and is not exactly as they appear.

This false online persona would go on to be labeled catfish, and which would also spawn a documentary and popular TV series (Wikipedia, 2020).

It's All in the Science

One of the greatest contributors to our understanding of the impact of social media is science. The science in seeing our reactions, deciphering the physiological reaction, and the hormones have made understanding the draw and the addiction of social media slightly easier to understand. In some research, there is a major focus on the MRI results of those who have displayed addictive behaviors towards social media, while other research looks at one's shift emotionally and psychologically.

Think of the popular Pavlovian theory, where popular scientist Ivan Pavlov looked at the correlated reaction of a stimulus. This concept is very much applicable to our understanding of social media addiction and dependency. Why? When we scroll through our Facebook, Twitter, or Instagram feed, anytime we encounter something that directly relates to us, our reward centers are triggered. The reward center of our brain releases dopamine, which is a "happy hormone," and as long as there is this hormonal release, we will continue to be drawn to finding more content that will fuel our reward center (Bergland, 2013).

This is a theory that has been tested time and time again in many labs around the world. Researchers have conclusively come to realize that the hold social media has on us and our life is very much linked to the release of the happy and euphoric feelings we desire. No one wants to be alone or to feel unwanted. Thanks to many of the social media platforms out there, no one ever has to feel alone or isolated, now they can venture into the digital and online world and find someone just like them.

This can be dangerous, however, especially if the common ideas and beliefs are about harming or illegal activities. Take for example, incels (involuntary celibates) who have taken to social media platforms to share their disdain for women. Around the world, there are tragic stories of terrorist attacks by this group of individuals who have found each other online. This is an unfortunate but true side of social media, which scientists and researchers have all linked to the wiring and development of the human mind (Haynes, 2018).

The Upside of Social Media — The Positive Benefits

Social media has this uncanny ability to link people who on the exterior may not have much in common but deep down, do. This is one of the great positives of social media. News stations from around the world often will share these feel good stories and how a simple post that has gone viral has brought happiness and joy to another person's life (Smart Social, 2018). For example, with COVID-19 impacting real life interaction, many people have been able to utilize different forms of social media to stay in contact with friends and family. People have been able to utilize chatting apps, video chats, and other forms of social media to safely catch up with loved ones. Utilizing social media in this way has been a great way for people to stay connected without the risk of in-person contact. Imagine having to go through such quarantine mandates before social media! Things would look a lot different indeed.

THIS is the positive side of social media, and it is a story that reminds many of us of the benefits social media has brought to society before it became complicated and a mental and psychological hindrance. While I often discuss Facebook, another platform that has shown to be a major boost in morale is Twitter.

Twitter has come a long way since its formation in 2006. It started off as a micro-blogging platform that allotted users a limit on the number of characters to use (Wojcik & Hughes, 2019). In the 14 years since its first launch, Twitter has also been used in a positive light. How so? Twitter allows its users to upload videos under a minute long and share and "like" the content. It may seem hard to understand how this is positive; however, Twitter has the ability to, in a matter of seconds, have a much faster reach than Facebook. Thanks to hashtags, lists, and followers, users can promote causes by resharing the content to their followers. For anyone who may not be familiar with or who may not understand Twitter, this can seem foreign; however, the best way to describe the reach of Twitter is to look at it like a domino. With each retweet and engagement, the more the message is reached.

The Benefits of Retweeting

While Facebook is commonly used to share stories, achievements, and more, Twitter has the ability to do all that and more. Twitter is also one of the few platforms out there that allows ordinary people to interact and engage with celebrities and those in the public eye. By tagging a certain person, you are drawing attention to your content and hoping that they too will find your content worth supporting and sharing with their own followers.

Re-tweeting as it is known, is where Twitter shows great positivity in sharing. As the saying goes, sharing is caring.

How Else is Social Media Positive?

Aside from sharing messages and content for a particular cause such as mental health, cancer, and social causes, social media offers more possibilities of positivity.

What other positive benefits come from social media?

The big one is exposure — exposure to a world that is unlike your own. For some, this can be the motivation to seek more than living in a small town, while for others, this is all they need. Social media has the ability to give those living in one part of the world the chance to virtually experience life on the other side of it. For example, someone in a small town in Lubbock, USA, may become friends with someone living in a small European town in Moldova. They can begin sharing parts of their lives and what it is like where they live. This could inspire the other to want to venture to their neck of the woods, or it could be simply a way to see what life is like and gain perspective.

Another way that social media offers positivity is it can actually be a teacher for self-development and growth. While I discuss aspects of how to disconnect and cope with the social anxiety of social media, there is an aspect of it that promotes growth.

How?

Look at the application Pinterest. This platform inspires users by trying something new, either a new recipe or project. While social media is commonly associated with sharing messages and causes, a fact that is often neglected is the educational aspect it provides users, especially those with very inquisitive minds. Another platform that encourages and supports learning and trying new things is YouTube, the video sharing platform. YouTube allows those who are skilled to share their knowledge with those looking to learn or try something, for example, playing guitar or learning how to dance.

We Can't Ignore the Positivity

While headlines often recognize the negativity and impact of social media on our well-being, we can't ignore the positivity that it has in the world. Social media has been a go-to for fundraisers to support forest fires, cancer research, and more. These cases of positivity deserve to be recognized because if it were not for that

Facebook post, that Twitter re-tweet, or Instagram like, we wouldn't know half of what we know.

Everything in life is about moderation, and this is very much a true statement when it comes to social media.

It can be so easy for us to negate the positivity and focus on the negatives; however, we shouldn't do that, or we will be pushing ourselves into this deep and often dark hole of seclusion. A lot has been accomplished thanks to the help of social media. From activism to fundraising, and even match making with a compatible partner. Since the rise in popularity, social media platforms have found ways of giving back and showing how their applications bring positivity.

Stop and think about a positive headline, about a cause, or how a veteran is honored for their services during Memorial Day. These are headlines that, while are plenty in number, are far from view to the public eye.

It is important that when we hear of the negative press, we remember the good it offers as well.

In this book, we discuss both because no story is complete without looking at the whole picture and understanding all angles.

How Social Media Has Promoted Connectedness

One of the ways that social media has promoted connectedness is through features such as video calling, instant messaging, and voice calls. While to some this may seem obvious, these are often underused and often underrated approaches of connecting. This is one of the ways that social media platforms are taking traditional methods to the next level. Platforms such as Facebook has a monopoly on WhatsApp and Instant Messenger allow for voice, video, and instant messaging.

Another way that social media has promoted connectedness is through the way they allow users to post and share content. Facebook is the most well-known platform and a pioneer in social media linking and connecting. The original purpose of Facebook, when it came to fruition in a dorm room at Harvard University, was to be a way of building a community and bringing people closer together. Though over the years and with its increased popularity and success, Facebook has become more than just an application for connecting people. The multi-functional application has evolved to be about promoting and sharing content, as well as connecting people from all parts of the world.

What Makes a Platform Ideal for Staying Connected?

When you think about Facebook and why this platform can't seem to be touched or be beaten, we have to look at the reach the platform has. Not only do you have to have a look at the reach but at how the platform is used. Nowadays, Facebook has expanded to allow users the ability to meet potential dating partners, post items to share, as well as create a networking community of professionals.

With each action, Facebook allows its users to share articles, personal opinions, as well as photos and videos. This type of engagement has allowed them to truly allow for that feeling of connectedness between people, even if they are oceans apart, but what is it about Facebook or any platform that gives this sense of belonging, of community? It is the real-time of our responses that allow for platforms such as Facebook, Snapchat, and Instagram to give us this feeling of connectedness. Even in different time zones, people can engage just as though they were right in front of the user posting the photos, videos, or content.

In a way, this real-time access to someone somewhere has allowed social media platforms to thrive. With many users thriving on and craving this connection, it does not matter whether the person responding or reacting was in the same city, state, zip code, or time zone. What matters most to the user is the reaction. This draw to social media is directly correlated to the effects it has on our hormones such as oxytocin, dopamine, and serotonin, or as medical researchers have dubbed them, the "happy hormones." Normally, our body releases these hormones when we see someone we love, when we get presents, or when something positive has happened; however, new research is showing that the happy hormones can be triggered by social media engagements.

Getting a "Like" is Equal to Falling in Love

It's such a bold statement to say that the "likes" we get on social media can equate to something as pure and passionate as falling in love, and yet, this is what researchers and professionals at Harvard, Yale, and MIT are discovering. Studies are showing that the positive engagement we receive, whether it's a comment or a "like," has the same effect on our body and mind as being in a relationship and in love. It is for this reason that social media is often regarded as being addictive, and at times it is even compared to being a drug for some.

Understanding the impact of social media on our physical and mental capacity can help us to make better decisions, but also to determine whether or not what we are doing is really sustainable. You may be telling yourself that there is no harm in checking your Twitter feed during a lunch break or procrastinating that book report to share videos of cute cats. The reality is, these small acts can snowball into something more. They can lay a foundation for behaviors that one doesn't want to possess.

Take for example this idea that the engagement and attention that social media gives is similar to being in love. Now, imagine if that relationship is one that is negative, that is abusive. Do you continue in that relationship even though you know it's bad for you? Do you allow yourself to be consumed by it or do you take a step back and take a break? Of course, it is easier said than done. Taking a break from social media can be as easy as deactivating your account temporarily (or permanently), while taking a break from a partner, or friend can be a bit more complicated; however, the emotions that are experienced between both are very similar. When you take a break from a friendship (romantic or not), you may find yourself rationalizing your behavior or your emotions, or even talking yourself back into the relationship. This same mindset can be said about social media and when you deactivate your account. You may tell yourself that you are going to not let it get to you or that you are going to block the negativity; however, this can only do so much and can only go so far.

Connected — Through Good and Bad

If we go back to the idea of social media being similar to a relationship, this idea of connectedness is very applicable. Social media is that relationship we want in a physical sense but virtually. Facebook, Twitter, Instagram, or Snapchat — these applications allow us to feel connected to those who share similar views, ideas, beliefs, but more importantly, they allow us to be wanted.

Social media, through good and bad, offers a link between those who do not feel as though they have someone, and this is something that is to be applauded when it comes to how social media has helped many people. It has given people a lifeline, but like with everything in life, moderation is best, excess is not.

All About the Clout

Another term that has come to be when it comes to social media is the word clout. No, this is not something that blocks our veins or arteries. Clout is defined as one's standards and ability to influence people (Tiffany, 2019). This is an example of how our connectedness with regards to social media is both good and bad. Clout is something that propels an individual to want to gain exposure and influence online.

There are applications and sites that can perform an analysis of one's online presence and rate their clout. The greater an online presence, the higher the clout they have. This pressure can make someone feel as though they have to share unique content or to be continually posting to gain more clout. While this is true, it only serves to fuel one's social media addiction even more.

Something that is sometimes forgotten about when dealing with a social media addiction is that what others think of you online truly doesn't matter in the grand scheme of things. Of course this is easier said than conceptualized; however, when you can associate the real world and those who we engage with versus those who we only speak to or chat with virtually, we can begin to realize this fact.

Do you remember in high school when there were the "cool kids" and the "not-so-cool kids?" Social media has, in a way, been able to replicate this via the many social media platforms, and clout is a prime example of this. Cool kids, or influencers as they are sometimes referred to, manage to draw in the everyday user and browser. They make them feel as though they too should be taking selfies non-stop, that they too should be posting around the clock.

Stop, and pause. You decide whether you want to take selfies or post non-stop, and remember, if you don't post a selfie, it doesn't mean people are going to unfriend you or ignore you.

Seeking Help Through Social Media

In this chapter, I have highlighted the good and bad of social media, as social media has demonstrated its power and influence over ordinary people. Despite everything, however, social media can provide an outlet for resources, and it can also be a form of reference for support.

Using Social Media for Support

The plus side of social media is that it can be a powerful resource for support groups and networks. Take for example someone looking to quit smoking, or a mother and wife who has left a relationship due to domestic violence. The internet, more specifically, social media, can provide information and guidance on various organizations that can help them. For many, social media provides the emotional and mental support that it takes to overcome addiction or abuse.

One way that social media has become a helpful tool for support is by the various applications and platforms. For example, some organizations allow their clients to fill out forms online that partners them up with mentors or assistants who would best suit their needs. In some cases, they can also virtually speak with someone. This is a major benefit for anyone who is embarrassed, afraid, or who wants to remain as anonymous as possible.

Why does anonymity matter when someone's trying to get help?

If someone is leaving an abusive relationship, speaking up may not be as easy to do as one would think. The person may feel shame, embarrassment, or they may feel like they can't speak up because no one can help them or protect them. With the option of a virtual chat that maintains anonymity, the person can seek the proper help and assistance they need.

Another added benefit to having a chat option is that there is virtual proof or evidence, which means if they need to get legal support or aid, they can take the transcript or the evidence with them.

However, for the most part, individuals who suffer from an addiction or mental health crisis are more likely to seek help when they feel they won't be judged. Chat rooms and seeking help virtually allow for this.

Empowering Patients Virtually

Did you know that sometimes the best support one can get is knowing that they are not alone? Cancer researcher Alexander Kirch (Wallner & Kirch, 2016), found that social media played a significant role in the treatment, coping, and acceptance of a patient's diagnosis. This meant that after a patient received a treatment or diagnosis, they were able to reach out to others with a similar cancer to seek support and guidance. Kirch highlighted the amazing impact social media had with their patients, with over 85% responding positively.

Further on in the cancer patient's treatment, Kirch found that patients turned to social media as a means of having open and honest discussions about treatments, support, alternative medicines, and cures. The most pivotal point for Kirch in the study of cancer patients was that nearly 60% of the 1,300 patients used social media as a form of feeling assured and hopeful.

Seeking Support BECAUSE of Social Media

While using social media for support and assistance is positive and beneficial, what happens if you need help because of social media? Then where do you turn to? What do you do when your usage becomes too much?

What do you do when your life becomes controlled by every "like," comment, or share?

When seeking support for one's dependency or excessive use of social media, there are a few options that can be considered. Still, the route will depend on how willing a person is to get the help they need.

It is important to remember that we are responsible for our decisions. We choose whether we want to allow something, such as social media, to control or dominate our lives and relationships (Skelly, 2012).

Recent studies have shown that some marriages that have ended have blamed social media for the demise of their relationship.

How?

It can highlight a couple's problems on a public platform. If a partner hides things or feels they may not be receiving the attention they deserve, they may turn to social media. Platforms, like Facebook, can bring unwanted opportunities of temptations.

These temptations are what have been known to lead to divorces.

Another way that social media has been known to lead to relationships ending is that it can test the trust between the couple. We discuss mental health and well-being, as well as anxiety and, in connection with that, trust can be something that is put to the test. For example, if a partner has self-esteem or trust issues, knowing that their partner has a Facebook or Instagram account may fuel their desire to constantly know who they are talking to, what they are posting, or even whose pictures they are liking. There have been known cases where two people have broken up because one person liked a photo they shouldn't have.

It is such a fine line sometimes because when you are in a relationship you want to trust the other person and you want to have transparency as well; however, at what point can we look at our own behavior and the behavior of our partner and say, that's not okay?

Social media has the ability to question the very foundation that relationships are built on, and because of this, relationship and marriage counselors have found themselves trying to support and facilitate relationships that are dealing with social media as a cause for friction.

Getting Help

The first step to seeking support for social media addiction and excess use is being open-minded about getting help. It means being aware that you may be spending more time online than offline with those around you. More importantly, it means looking around at the relationship you have and seeing how your actions online or rather offline are being affected by your use of social media.

Once you have taken on this first step of acknowledgment, then you can begin the process of looking for and seeking the proper help. If however, one is unable to admit to their excessive use or the impact it has on them or those around them, seeking help may not be ideal. Why? Think of it like this, people who genuinely want help are going to do their part to help the process; however, if the person is unwilling, they may only give a half-hearted attempt to fix things.

If you think you have a problem, or if you know someone who does, reflect on this thought: If you spend more time on your phone or smart device than you do engaging with real people, there may be a problem.

Now, if you are prepared to get help, such help can come in the form of speaking with a therapist, counselor, or support group. Each type provides its own pros and cons.

A therapist and counselor are great for anyone comfortable and open to talking. Thankfully, nowadays, sessions can be held virtually and from the comfort of the patient's home. This can be a perk as it allows the individual to feel safe and more willing to be open. Sometimes being somewhere that is a safe place can be all the support one needs, especially if they may feel embarrassed about speaking with or getting help from a medical professional.

Support groups are a great form of help. Typically support groups work well for those who feel they need to have others who can understand and relate to what they are going through. Many other addictions, such as alcohol and gambling, use support groups to overcome addiction or habit.

Knowing that others are experiencing what you are also experiencing is sometimes a great relief. Sometimes, it's nice to see that you aren't alone and that, like you, they too want to get the help they need to live a better and fuller life.

Chapter 3:

Designed for Your Attention

"The reason many people are on social media is because they want attention. It's measured by the number of likes, views, retweets,comments, etc. Remember, you don't have to rely on others for your confidence and self-esteem. Disengage from seeking attention. Love yourself first." - Mufti Menk

When an application like ChatRoulette came onto the world wide web, people questioned its validity. Many thought that an application that paired you randomly with people around the world would flounder; however, it turns out that this application would go on to be worth nearly 30 million dollars. ChatRoulette, was the brainchild of a 17-year-old Russian who was intrigued by the movie and became inspired to create an application that would allow users to interact with random people around the world.

This is a prime example of how a platform was designed to draw in the public's intrigue and curiosity. Though ChatRoulette would be popular for a few years, it would find its downfall when users violated the code of conduct by showing and engaging in lewd behavior. The application would also find itself under scrutiny by parent groups who found under-age users were being groomed by older users of the application. Again, this just goes to demonstrate how a successful social media platform has, in one way or another, found itself under the magnifying glass of the media.

Social media platforms are designed to not only attract users but they are meant to push the boundaries. In 2020, many parts of the world found themselves under quarantine and isolated. While many would think that this would impact any new possible application's growth, it did not. Far from it, Instagram and OnlyFans would partner together to create a phenomenon that would give those in isolation a new form of entertainment and social media platform. What differentiates OnlyFans from existing ideas and most social media platforms is that this application is commonly used for adult performers and is often associated with adult-only content. Just when you think that every possible idea of a social media platform has been thought of, enter OnlyFans. The application is founded by British Tim Stokely, who, like the former application, ChatRoulette, has found himself under fire for exploiting users and those who turn to OnlyFans to make income.

Whether one agrees or disagrees, one cannot deny the massive draw a scandal or celebrity endorsement has on the platform. As the saying goes, any attention is good attention. With social media creators, any traction their platform gets brings more potential users and subscribers.

For Every High, There is a Fall

What happens when people find themselves with double-digit social media accounts? What happens when they find themselves victims of their own obsession and compulsive desire to be popular, wanted, and liked? What happens when the worst-case scenario of meeting someone online becomes real?

This is one of the biggest downfalls and unfortunate dangers of social media. It is both pleasant and positively affirming, but it can also be toxically negative. For early adopters of social media, typically those who fall under Millennials' classification, they know these dangers more than other users of social media.

Why? Michael Dimock of Pew Research Centre (Dimock, 2019) labels Millennials as anyone born between 1981 to 1996. It is this age group that has been the most impacted by social media. This is the age group that has contributed to the research of looking at the impact prolonged screen time has on the mind and well-being. It is this same age group that has been the driving force in understanding how social media can be both appealing and repulsive all in one. This is also the age group where users have either removed themselves entirely from the platform or have become casual users of specific applications. They may use social media to stay in touch with family and friends or for professional purposes, but their outward activity is limited.

Following the Money

While millennials contribute significantly to the research and understanding of social media and its value, they are massive financial contributors to it as well. It is because of this that many platforms have evolved to what they are now.

Initially, many platforms such as Twitter and LinkedIn required users to pay a membership fee. This made it exclusive to anyone who had the financial means and wanted to be part of the digital community enough to want to pay for the added perks (Lieberman, 2007). Interestingly enough, this same group of individuals felt that social media should not be charging people to use their platforms. These features that they once paid monthly and yearly fees have become free and accessible to all.

One of the things that has been shown to be successful for many social media platforms is understanding the desires, wants, and needs of their market.

If we look at Facebook, we know that they allow and endorse free speech. Still, at the same time, they know that if they create a platform that is a one-stop-shop, users will encourage and advocate others to join the platform. In the last few years, Facebook has evolved to include a Marketplace that allows its users to sell, trade, and exchange items with fellow users.

The significance?

Using an already established platform such as Facebook and having its already verified members list and sell items means that they can trust the person on the receiving or rather selling end. Yes, there may be the occasional scam or fake account; however, for the most part, Facebook Marketplace allows its users to verify and check the seller or buyer before any transaction takes place.

Smart Marketing

Every year during the Superbowl, the main attraction was not the teams who played, but rather the commercials and halftime show. Since the creation and rise of social media platforms, not only brands, but also special events such as the Superbowl have gone on to find ways of integrating various platforms for their gain.

Thanks to Snapchat, there are geographically based filters that users can select from and apply to their photos. Some filters are sponsored, while others are not, but of course, the money comes from the filters that are sponsored or tagged by a company. This strategic marketing is what draws users and what fuels people's constant desire to stay connected.

While Snapchat offers sponsored filters, Instagram offers hashtags that continue to spread the company's name and brand. Still, it can sometimes result in the user receiving attention. As discussed in previous chapters and in future chapters, the awareness that one gets on social media can be both positive and negative, but what can't be forgotten is that it's all about marketing. As we said earlier, any press is good press, which is most definitely true for social media.

For Every "Like," There is a "Dislike" to Social Media

Go anywhere in the world, and chances are you are going to see in their constitution the freedom of free speech. While this is commonly associated with the spoken word, it applies to the written word as well. This is where social media can get complicated and messy because for every "like" and for every person that agrees with your point of view, there are a handful of dislikes and those willing to challenge your thoughts and views.

Again, this is one of the biggest appeals of social media, and why platforms such as Facebook have billions of users, with millions more signing up each day.

The Business Model for Social Media — A Billion Dollar Industry

There is no denying that social media platforms like Facebook, Twitter, Instagram, and Tik Tok are worth millions. However, if you look at how they are utilized, there is no denying they are a billion-dollar industry. What makes these addicting and appealing platforms worth so much?

Their consumers, their memberships, their users, THEY are the ones who fuel their successes. Every time a user recruits another friend or shares a product or message, it pushes the platform further into the masses. This approach is a double-edged sword. Look at how we have discussed the negative (and positive) impact of social media on our mental and physical well-being. If you look at how many of these companies started off, they began with private investors and advertisers willing to take a chance on advertising with them, many of them hoping their users would come to their services if they saw the advertising. Though this approach is still very much true, it has become much more prevalent and apparent. When you browse through your Facebook newsfeed, you can find advertising that is more often than not specialized to *your* interests and needs. This is the jackpot for these businesses; however, herein lies the problem with social media.

Social media pries into your inner desires and wants, even when you think they are not. They get a hold of what you want, and they intensify the need, show you how you are missing out and why you should "invest" in a particular product or service. Forever utilizing the "advertisement paid for," these social media companies are finding ways of monetizing each click and impression. This approach to monetizing every exposure means that Facebook, Instagram, and Snapchat have to do nothing but allow for the marketing, and this approach is indeed making them billions of dollars.

Customer Relationships and Innovation

Two factors that all social media platforms share are customer relationships and innovation. These contribute to the success of a business and force its users to continually be drawn in and willing to either continue their subscription or invest in products.

The partnership of Instagram and OnlyFans is one example of how a multi-million-dollar company, Instagram, found a way to appeal to their adult-only users while also turning a profit. This partnership is also a form of innovation. Two individual social media platforms have come together; however, this is a practice that is becoming quite common for successful companies. For example, if you search on Facebook and the companies and shares it holds, you will find that some companies and brands are owned by Facebook. This practice of having a monopoly in the industry is common practice in many industries; the only difference is these don't often have such an impact on its users.

When Microsoft buys out smaller tech firms, it doesn't negatively impact one's self-esteem or mental well-being. When a social media giant like Facebook invests in other social media platforms, you can always expect there to be repercussions for the users.

What Repercussions?

Users can feel the pressure of what these platforms expect of them. If we look back at OnlyFans, there is an expectation that the users will be physically attractive and not the girl or guy-next-door appeal. Sure, this is maybe someone's appeal; however, sex sells, and the imagination of perfection is what appeals and draws people in.

Regulating Social Media - Is it Possible?

When you see a plate of cookies, are you able to eat just one?

When you see chocolate or candy, can you restrain yourself from finishing the whole bag, or do you just give in to temptation?

Think of social media like our cravings, temptations, and addictions. There will be times regulation is easy and possible; however, there will also be times when it is hard and downright impossible.

Why?

For the same reason that we can't say no to another piece of the pie or another bite of the chocolate bar. It fuels the happy centers of our brain to make us crave it more and more (McSweeney, 2019). In a way, this is what continually drives people to frequently check their Facebook and Twitter feed. It is also the reason why some find it essential, if not a daily part of their routine, to post updates on what they are doing, eating, or how their relationship is going (or not going). Social media draws its user in the same way an alcoholic, shopaholic, or foodie is drawn in.

All-or-Nothing Regulation

Though health professionals all agree that regulation is essential, there is still debate about how much of it is good enough (Robinson & Smith, 2020). According to some health professionals, specifically those who interact with teens and young adults, social media is a significant cause of mental and emotional disorders. Take, for example, teens who struggle with body dysmorphia and are in constant need of reassurance and validation. Social media platforms such as Facebook, Instagram, Snapchat, and TikTok, provide this boost in confidence.

That's good, right?

No, and this is because it fosters a vicious cycle that can be hard to break from. It may even lead down a rabbit hole of more problems. This is where health professionals struggle to agree upon what is appropriate regulation and how to regulate it in situations where the individual's entire life is controlled by it.

Though the doctors and therapists may still be up in the air about what is considered a good amount of social media, we can conclude that some form of regulation is needed to ensure a proper balance in one's mental and emotional well-being (Pantic, 2014).

What Can I Do?

Do you find that your life is completely dominated and controlled by social media?

Have you noticed a difference in your demeanor and the relationships in your life?

When you put your phone down or disconnect for a couple of hours or days, do you find that you begin to get anxious about missing out?

If you answered yes to any of the previous statements, maybe it is time to take a break and address the fact that you may be nearing a social media addiction.

It is not as bad as it sounds; if anything, the fact that you are able to recognize and be honest with yourself is a massive step because, so often, people who spend too much time online or who share too much information refuse to acknowledge or recognize this fact. If you can look at yourself in the mirror and realize that you should probably cut back on your screen time or that maybe you are allowing yourself to be controlled by the opinions of those you've never met in person, this is a step in the right direction.

Quick Tips

Consider the following recommendations for a list of quick suggestions on how to address your social media addiction.

Time Restrictions

One of the best things you can do to address your social media addiction (or potentially soon-to-be addiction) is to set time restrictions. Setting a time restriction helps us put into perspective just how much time we spend online rather than on things that need to be addressed. A time restriction works if you have the discipline and can self-regulate; however, if you struggle to hold yourself accountable, this may not be ideal.

If you are up for the challenge, iOS and Android applications can be downloaded to help set and stick to time restrictions. Once downloaded, create your settings and begin the journey to cutting back on social media, and see if you can stick to a time limit.

Deactivate and Disconnect

Quitting an addiction 'cold turkey' is a drastic approach for those who want immediate action. Many have benefitted from this approach with great success. It's both possible to do and effective. Many will deactivate and disconnect entirely from social media, with some never returning to the platforms they've left behind.

A downfall with deactivating and disconnecting is the peer-pressure one may feel from their friends as well as themselves. When a friend doesn't support your choice to "quit" social media, it can be hard to deal with, let alone follow through. It is for this reason having support is *always* essential. You don't even have to justify or explain why you are leaving or taking a break from social media, just that you are and want their support.

Time Tracking

If you have an iOS device, did you know that you can track your screen time? At the end of every week, you will receive a notification that will tell you how much time was spent browsing. Once it has determined a baseline through algorithms, it will then inform you whether you are spending more or less time on the device.

Androids and iOS devices also have the ability to track how much of your time is spent on a particular application. Why is this helpful? Sometimes seeing the numbers in front of our eyes can help us be aware of the amount of time we "waste" on Snapchat, Facebook, and the like. For many people, seeing how much time is spent or lost browsing is enough to curb their usage.

A way of combating certain addictions is to face what it is that is "ruining" our lives because it requires us to be honest and vulnerable. Both are neither easy nor pleasant to own up to.

Simplify Your Life

Sometimes the best way to avoid temptation is to remove the temptation itself. If you find yourself browsing the Twitter feed more than you care to admit, delete the application. Deleting applications that distract you is the best way to stay focused. Nowadays, many devices have multiple functions, but this multifunctionality is what is known to distract and create more problems down the road.

Simplify your life! Remember, life was simple at one point, and we were not prisoners of our smart devices.

Set Goals

Why do you want to cut back or cut out social media? Is it ruining your relationships? Is it affecting your performance at work?

When you can identify your goals and the purpose of putting a stop to your aimless wandering online, you can achieve them. Goal-setting is a common approach used by counselors and therapists working with clients who are addicted to and want to stop their social media addiction (Eisenberger & Lieberman, 2005). So often, social media users don't realize they are addicted until someone else points it out. This can be a good thing, but it can also be a bad thing. It's good that someone has the courage to be honest with us about our use of social media; however, it can be bad if we don't want to recognize or acknowledge our addiction or if we are not ready to do so.

It's a Process

Awareness of the design and appeal of social media is one thing. Learning to step back and step away is a process. It is a process that does not happen right away, and it is one that requires constantly checking in and readdressing the goals, expectations, and limits.

Yes, social media provides us with news about current events and keeps us connected; however, it does not mean it should, by all means, control us or shape who we are. Don't give up on becoming a better person, and don't feel like you are alone. Social media affects hundreds, if not thousands of people every day in the US (Dimock, 2019).

Chapter 4:

Is There *REALLY* a Problem?

"If social media controls you and is robbing you of your freedom and good emotional energy chances are you're addicted and it's time to find another hobby." - Germany Kent

Perhaps you think that social media addiction is a strongly worded phrase. That's because it is. Addiction, no matter what it is to, is a serious problem. It can control your life and your behavior, whether you realize it or not.

You may suspect that you have a problem with social media but not know how much effect it has on you. Going through this chapter, you will be able to understand just how many ways a social media addiction can touch your life. While reading, if several topics sound like your experiences, you may very well have an addiction.

Understanding whether or not you have a problem is an excellent stepping stone for moving forward. You may not think you have an addiction, only to realize you actually do. Recognize that there is no shame in admitting you have a problem. In fact, it takes real bravery to acknowledge it to yourself and to others. In many cases, addiction is seen as a disease that you are not expected to fight alone. You may be surprised by how much your family and friends are willing to support you and help you work through it.

Additionally, knowing the areas of your life that are impacted gives you a more straightforward path. When you see where the problems lie, you can understand how to go about fixing them.

Cognitive and Behavioral Effects

The frequent use of social media can have significant effects on your cognitive and behavioral actions. You probably don't even realize that your thoughts and decisions are conditioned to respond in a very specific way.

When you first venture out into the social media world, many of your actions may be due to organic thought. However, over time, you will see that your social media habits influence the sites you visit, the things you post, and the purchases you make.

Reinforcement of Thoughts, Opinions, Views and Biases

When you post, "share", or "like" something it can be a statement. Does it tell a story? Does it reveal your political point of view? It is usually a good thing to have a point of view, and even better to have the self-confidence to share that opinion. However, when your posts, "likes", and "shares" display a recurring theme of one perspective, it can lead you down a road of trouble.

Having your own point of view is excellent, but part of being a well-rounded person means you are open to listening to someone else's opinion. This requires you to be exposed to another person's unique perspectives. Unfortunately, it can be hard to do this when you only browse and post things that reflect your opinion. Any "likes" and positive reactions you receive end up reinforcing your point of view and can even narrow it. It makes you feel empowered, and as though your perspective is the right one. Others may even feel hesitant to post anything contrary to you, fearing the potential backlash.

The content of your posts can also narrow the field of commentators. People tend to react to posts that they genuinely like. This means that only those who have the same opinion as you are going to like your perspective-based posts. When conversations around your posts begin, they are likely going to reinforce your views. Your thoughts get backed up because other people are agreeing with you. And while it is nice to find agreement amongst friends, it can make you quite biased to an opposing view.

Being biased is a problem when you refuse to hear the opinions of others. You don't have to agree with someone else to listen to their point of view. But you do need to understand that there is more than one side to every story. You don't even need to agree with someone in order to be friends. Learning to tolerate and accept different points of view is essential for living in harmony (Andersen, 2015).

Post Content

Have you ever posted something online that you would never normally do in person? That is the effect social media has on your cognitive actions.

When you make a post, what is your goal? The answer is probably to get as many "likes" as possible. And through experience, you likely know that posts with the most provocative actions or words tend to get the most "likes" and "shares." This drives you to post things you would never do in any other public arena.

Social media can condition you to post risque content. Some researchers have likened it to Pavlov's Dog's experiment, where he conditions a set of dogs to salivate upon hearing a bell ring. Instead of a bell, "likes," comments, and "shares" are the reinforcement you get when you post content. Since you enjoy the attention you get, you continue to post more and more.

Consumer Behavior

What you buy and what you search out online can be influenced by your social media habits. Influencers and ads pop up in your feed precisely because of what you post and what you look up. Businesses can pay to track your browsing history so that the ads on the side of your screen are particularly attractive to you.

Ever wonder why you start seeing ads for bed sheets after looking them up on Amazon? It's not a coincidence. Businesses buy that information to be able to draw you in with deals and advertisements. Through experience, companies know that you are more likely to make a purchase when it pops up on your screen like this.

If you find you make more online purchases now than ever before, analyze your behavior. Are you making those purchases because you need to or because you want to? Has your spending increased to the point that you are teetering on spending more than you can afford? Look back at your social media use and see if those things are linked. You may be surprised to learn how often you make purchases because of social media advertisements.

Attention Disorders

Numerous studies have been done to see if social media and phone use are linked to attention disorders (Skelly, 2012). While no current study specifically concludes a connection, they do show that more research is needed into the subject. This conclusion has been reached because many symptoms associated with attention disorders are also linked to spending too much time on socials.

Attention disorder symptoms that may sound familiar to you include:

- Difficulty paying attention to one task

- Hyperactivity
- A constant feeling of restlessness
- Difficulty sitting still to focus
- Lack of impulsivity controls

Attention disorders can be problematic for kids and teens in school. Traditional learning environments can be particularly tricky, as can traditional workplaces. While it is possible to treat symptoms with therapy, medication, and accommodations, living with an attention disorder can be quite challenging.

Even though there is no proven link between social media and attention disorders, some researchers believe that it should be a cause for concern. If you experience any of the above symptoms, evaluating your social media use may be the right decision.

Physical Effects

It is easy to assume that social media problems are often only associated with mental health and social issues. Many people forget or don't realize that their physical health can be affected, too. Just like mental health problems, the physical ones can be severe, especially if they go too long unaddressed. Physical health problems do not show up overnight. They are long-running body stressors that begin as a small issue and develop into larger problems.

Not addressing or recognizing the impact that social media has on our physical body can sometimes be grave.

Sleep Problems

Sleep is a crucial part of your physical and mental well-being. Sleep gives your mind and body time to rest and regenerate. Most adults need anywhere between six and eight hours of sleep per night in order to function correctly. Social media can very quickly get in the way of good sleep.

Firstly, you may find yourself lying in bed on your phone late into the night. Your intent was to go to bed on time, even earlier than normal, but you get sucked into the social media vortex. Before you know it, an hour has passed, and you haven't got any rest yet. Unfortunately, you may not even feel tired anymore because your brain has been working so hard to pay attention to your screen that you are now running on overdrive.

Secondly, social media can cause a serious problem for night wakers. If you wake up between sleep cycles, you may reach for your phone when you can't fall right back to sleep. Unfortunately, this does you more harm than good. The blue light on your phone and the information displayed on your newsfeed causes your brain to awaken fully, even when it is not ready. This means you are going to have even more trouble getting back to sleep.

If you regularly experience these situations, social media is probably getting in the way of achieving a good night's rest.

Fatigue

Fatigue is very closely related to not getting enough sleep, but it is a problem all on its own. If you do not get enough sleep at night, then you likely experience fatigue during your work or school day. Fatigue means you will have trouble concentrating on a task at hand because your brain is so tired. Additionally, you may feel cranky, causing you to be in a poor mood throughout the day. All of this can then, in turn, affect your communication with bosses, coworkers, friends, and teachers.

Fatigue can also cause problems when driving. When you are driving, you are responsible not only for yourself but for all other lives on the road. Many accidents have been caused by people falling asleep at the wheel. Fatigue is a very dangerous thing to experience while driving.

When your social media use causes you to experience fatigue, the physical ramifications can be quite severe.

Eye Strain

Eyes are not designed to stare at a screen all day, especially not a very small one like your phone. When you spend so much time browsing through social media, your eyes can experience strain.

The strain on your eyes may lead to severe enough problems so as to need glasses. It can also cause headaches and even migraines. Unfortunately, once you lose your eyesight, there is no getting it back.

Eye strain may be a significant problem for people who work on a computer all day long. Then you come home and continue to look at the screen. Exposing your eyes to that type of light all day every day is usually a problem for most people.

Carpal Tunnel Syndrome

Musculoskeletal issues are common for anyone who does a repetitive task. Moving your body in the same way in the same position over and over can cause physical pain. A common one of these injuries is Carpal Tunnel Syndrome.

Carpal Tunnel Syndrome affects your hands and/or wrists and is caused by spending too much time typing. It is even worse if you type in the wrong position. An ergonomically designed chair and desk can help alleviate it, but many people type on social media from their bed or couch.

A form of Carpal Tunnel Syndrome can also be caused by keying with your fingers on your phone. It does not necessarily have to come from a computer.

Carpal Tunnel Syndrome can be an occupational hazard, or the result of student activities. It would be wrong to suggest it solely as a result of social media addiction, but the obsession does nothing to help the problem.

Lack of Exercise

When you spend a lot of your free time on social media, you have less time for other things in your life. One of the most important things you can do for your physical health is exercise. For many people, training is one of the first things to go when their time is limited.

While lack of exercise is bad for your physical health, it also affects your mental health. Your mind and body are connected, so when you don't treat your body with respect, your mind also suffers. Taking care of your body with regular exercise helps to stave off serious health issues. While it cannot solve everything, most doctors recommend eating a balanced diet and getting regular exercise. When social media gets in the way of this advice, you may have a problem.

Distraction

Social media has a way of drawing in your whole mind. It is so impressive that it makes it nearly impossible to multitask; this includes browsing and walking.

Most people have seen videos of what happens when you are buried in your phone while walking. Maybe you watched as someone walked right into a pole or a fountain, or perhaps they walked right past their significant other without noticing them. Whatever the case, being immersed in your phone can have serious physical consequences.

Distraction also comes into play when being on your phone while driving. Many places have created laws against it, but people still engage in this behavior every single day.

If you recently decided to pick up your phone to check your social media while driving, you may have a serious addiction problem.

Posture

Phone screens are small. Even though they have a very clear picture, they still need to be held close to the face to see them properly. Unfortunately, this is not a natural position to be in.

Often, your arms are held high while your head is bent down. This position causes your neck to strain forwards. In turn, your shoulders round forwards, as well. Being in this position for extended hours can cause lasting damage to your posture. Poor posture can lead to problems as you age, including back and neck pain.

These are just a few of the most commonly known impacts that social media has on our physical well-being. There are other impacts that it has, some much more severe than others.

For example, those who consider themselves adrenaline junkies or thrill seekers may push their bodies to the limit and take risks just to get that perfect photo or "likes" not realizing that every time they bungee, or they reach new heights, their body is worn down faster.

It's more than physical...

In a way, for the social media addict, adrenaline is something they run on. They run on the thrill and the possibility that their next adventure is going to be a massive hit, that they are going to become influencers or trend setters. While one can wish and hope, this is not always the case. In reality, there are more cases of people who don't become influencers than there are.

Does this matter to a social media addict?

No, because addicts - social media, substances, whichever vice you choose - thrive on the premise that there is a possibility. In a way, it is more of a falsehood than anything. An addict who refuses to acknowledge their role, or negates the impact of social media on their lives is the hardest to convince.

Why?

Because no one wants to believe that they are an addict. No one wants to think that the very thing that brings them such pleasure and joy is what is harming their real-life relationships and physical well-being. It is easier to deny the truth than accept it. It is for this reason that when it comes to addressing one's social media addiction, acknowledgment and acceptance play such a large role in the treatment.

Impact on Interpersonal Relationships

Online relationships are very different from in-person relationships. Online, you can be whoever you want, especially if you have never met the other person face-to-face. Behind a screen, you can speak your true opinion, engage in your deepest fancy, or simply be yourself. However, it's hard for someone else to know what side of you is being represented. All of this makes online interpersonal relationships incredibly confusing.

Online Relationships - False by Design

When we forge relationships on social media, can we really determine how real or authentic they are? Is the person you are talking to showing their genuine self? Are you?

On social media, most people only post the very best version of what is going on in their lives. It is a false descriptor of what their real life looks like. Most people don't spend their weekends in posh hotels by the pool, eating grapes from a silver platter while wearing a sequin gown. However, if you scroll through their social media, you may believe that is the case.

Trouble arises when online friends have deeper connections. It is problematic when neither person knows much about the other. You only see the version they choose to present. By comparison, with an in-person relationship, you can get to know a person very quickly when you see how they interact with their family, strangers, or even how they react to a stressful situation. All of this learning is lost in online relationships.

Perhaps the most upsetting part of this is that you may never know until you finally meet in person. You could spend years of your life thinking you are talking to someone only to find out they are not at all how they represented themselves. Realizations like this can be emotionally and mentally destructive.

Seeking Drama

Drama is often about attention. In order to get more attention, you need to create some drama. Social media is the ideal place to find attention. Someone is always online, willing to give their opinion, good or bad. You may be so starved for attention that you don't care whether the reaction is positive or negative, as long as someone notices you.

All humans need attention; it is a natural part of human connection. This is one reason people end up posting their entire lives on Facebook, Twitter, Instagram, and Snapchat. They are looking for others to give them reinforcement. This is another reason people choose only to post the best or juiciest parts of their life. They want, and need, the reactions from others.

A lot of this attention and drama-seeking is people wanting to feel like they belong. Feeling isolated from others is gut-wrenching and causes people to post their entire lives, or versions of it, all over social media. The whole purpose behind it is to feel some sort of connection to others, to know that someone cares about what you are going through.

Bullying

Bullying is a problem that has existed for many years. It used to be that a person got bullied in the schoolyard, but could then escape to the tranquility of their home. That is no longer true. Now, the bully lives in your pocket, following you everywhere you go.

Online bullying is a serious problem. It is so severe that suicide rates are at an all-time high. Many suicides have been attributed to bullying through social media. When someone feels so attacked that they live in a place of despair, they may turn to suicide to ease the pain. It is important to recognize that not all bullying leads to death from suicide. However, that does not make it any better.

Online bullying is unique because it can go on secretly forever. Parents and teachers usually do not have full access to what's going on with a child's social media. Messages sent can be deleted instantly, so no one but the recipient and sender knows what was said. Additionally, messages can be sent from numerous platforms, so there is no escape. Finally, messages can even be sent from fake accounts. There are so many ways to be bullied online that it is hard to keep track.

Many people associate bullying with school-aged children and teenagers. But it can exist for adults too, in the social media world. It works the exact same way. Unwanted messages are sent to your accounts from people who take pleasure in tormenting you. Their goal is to find some sort of personal satisfaction in tearing you down. Bullying hurts at any age and should never be taken lightly.

If you are being bullied online, or you are the bully, you may have problems with social media. Getting help specifically for bullying may be an excellent choice for you. Don't ever be afraid to confide in someone if you are being bullied. Friends and family are there to help.

Impact on Communication Skills

Social media was invented as a means of communication. It has provided many users with the ability to communicate with friends and family around the world. Socials offer a platform for making new friends and connecting with old ones. They have even been responsible for many marriages. All of this makes it sound as though social media is a beautiful place. And while it can be, it also has a very negative effect on people's communication skills.

Knowing what to say and how to be...

While social media can prove beneficial, the hindrance on one's interpersonal skills can sometimes make it hard for one to have meaningful and relatable relationships. It can impact one's ability to know how to engage in person, and it can sometimes, as previously stated, provide a sense of falsehood that is not easily noticeable if not acceptable.

In the same breath, I think it is also important to recognize that social media can benefit many in a way that, had it not been for their creation, people would not have discovered their talents or their skills. For example, think of the memes, the GIFs, and the emojis we use in our dialogues. These came to be because someone was able to harness their creativity and put it to use; hence, helping others in expressing themselves.

Again, this just goes to highlight how, even in social media, for every upside there is a downside.

Limiting of Characters Encourages the Expression of Negative Emotion

Social media sites, like Twitter, specifically, limit the number of characters you are able to use. Interestingly, this restriction can result in a change in messaging. When your ability to express your opinion is limited, it becomes necessary to get your point across without the full context. Unlike with other mediums, you do not have the option to give background about your post. This means your post can come across harsher and more direct than you may intend.

Thoughts and opinions are complex ideas. They are formed based on personal experience and values. However, when you post something on Twitter, you cannot completely explain your thoughts. Your space is so limited that if you are mildly upset about something, it may come across as though you are infuriated. This can cause a problem, creating misunderstandings and arguments between you, friends, family, and even strangers.

The online world is a place of heavy debate. When characters are limited, it can make this even worse. So often, people use words of hate and anger to get their point across. Others then read and retaliate, leading to what has become known as a *Twitter War*. Instead of being able to have a healthy debate, people engage in brutal arguments that end up being more of a personal attack than anything else.

Debate is, in fact, a very good thing in society. It leads to the progression of opinions and moves nations forward. However, to make this possible, both sides have to be willing to hear the other. They need to be open to listening to another opinion and considering it valid. This conversation structure is often lost in Twitter wars when everyone weighs in. They may not have anything constructive to contribute, but they put their thoughts out there just because they can. While everyone is entitled to their opinion, it is often not what you say but how you say it that gets your point across. This nuance can be lost when character space is limited.

Impact on Language Skills

Over the years, social media has changed the way people communicate with each other; it has even changed parts of the English language. People converse over their screens now as the primary form of communication. It used to be that people spent time with each other at the mall, going to a park, or on the phone. Now, individuals prefer to stay home and communicate from behind a screen. This is why there are effects on language, vocabulary, and articulation.

The English language has been permanently affected by social media. Everyone is familiar with terms like *selfie* and *meme*. Before socials, these words did not exist at all. Now, they are part of the mainstream language, even existing in the Oxford Dictionary. Social media is so powerful that it is responsible for inventing words!

English has also been changed by giving new meanings to already existing words. For example, the word *catfish* has been around for decades. Before social media, it referred to the bottom feeder fish that is considered a culinary delicacy in some places around the world. Now, *catfish* also means a person who disguises themselves under a fake profile in order to communicate with someone. This example proves how much authority social media has over the way we communicate with each other.

Social media also has affected people's vocabulary and writing skills. Socials have their own style of talking, including short forms such as *ttyl, brb, nsfw,* and *cus*. When you spend so much of your time online using these terms, you are limiting your exposure to other, more traditional forms of writing.

Like anything else, increased exposure means you learn more about a given subject. People who spend more time reading books and articles tend to have a greater vocabulary pool. They also tend to understand and use proper grammar. People who spend a lot of time using online jargon may lose out on that skill. They are exposed to a different type of language, so use the online terms instead. This can be particularly problematic when you need to write documents at work or produce papers for school. Your language, vocabulary, and grammar may be limited.

Another problem you may face is difficulty expressing yourself. Articulation of emotions can be challenging at any given time, but social media may make it even more difficult. Interestingly, you may find that you are able to express yourself online but not in person. Being behind a screen tends to give people more courage to express themselves. It may even be easier given the endless options of emojis. However, doing so in person is not the same. When you only learn how to articulate your emotions online, you may not even know how to do it in person.

Adults vs. Children

The developmental years of a person's life can be dramatically affected by the use of social media. What they see and how they interact with friends and influencers can shape them well into their adult lives. Though the real impact of growing up with social media is yet to be discovered, there are many factors parents and researchers worry about.

Individuals are joining social media earlier and earlier. This means more of their formative years are coupled with having a social media profile. Their self-worth, values, and actions may all be affected by what they see and experience online. The "likes" they receive and conversations with others can dramatically impact their overall emotional and mental development.

One of the most challenging things to deal with is bullying. Many teens experience bullying, as outlined earlier in this chapter. A significant problem with bullying is that the effects do not go away once the taunting stops. People hold on to that well into adulthood. Choices they make, people they encounter, the way they act at the grocery store, all of those things can be controlled by bullying in their developmental years. Bullying is toxic behavior that needs to be dealt with as soon as possible. The unfortunate thing is that it can go undetected for years on social media, making self-esteem issues so much worse.

Social media can also cause significant peer pressure. When a teen sees others behaving a certain way, they want to follow suit. It is natural to want to fit in with the 'cool' group. That desire is as old as time. However, it is much harder to resist when kids are on social media. Not only do they hear the pressure from peers, but they see it with their own eyes. Teens may post photos from the latest house party where they are smoking drugs and drinking alcohol, followed by tons of "likes." The desire to get in on the action and receive the same attention can lead to kids participating in behavior they wouldn't typically.

Social media friends and influencers can also cause a teen to get an unrealistic view of life. Since people only post glamorous photos, people seeing this in their developmental years may believe this is how life is supposed to be. Assuming this can result in teens thinking their life is not good enough. It can inspire jealousy or disdain for their own lives. It may also be harmful to their self-esteem because they believe their life is not as good or exciting as those they follow online.

The adverse effects of social media on kids and teens can be quite damaging. But does social media affect adults the same way?

The short answer is yes. Even a well-developed adult brain can be affected by what it sees on social media. It can cause low self-esteem, instill jealousy, and even bullying. While social media can have some excellent aspects, such as keeping in touch with friends from afar, it can be very harmful as well.

Impact on the Brain

Social media has long been suspected of causing issues with a person's brain. Regular use of social media can indeed create problems for people. Reading on, you may recognize that some of the following factors have impacted your life. You may experience one or several of these issues. The more you have encountered, the more you may be struggling with a social media addiction.

Turns You into a Follower

Some people are followers by nature, some are leaders, and yet others fall somewhere in the middle. Even the most independent thinker can turn into a follower because of the influence social media has on your brain.

Social media is an example of herd mentality. It shows you what is popular at the time. Due to the fact that you see the same image or thoughts over and over, you may begin to believe it is true. Even if you disagree with it, you may feel scared to state your opinion because of potential repercussions. The court of public opinion can be a terrifying place for anyone who disagrees with the majority. Especially online, where people feel they are free to use strong, sometimes hurtful, language.

This is not to say that being a follower is bad; however, I am trying to demonstrate that sometimes, following the masses is not always best. The herd mentality can be a dangerous thing. Look at the many online trends that, at the time, were probably really good; however, like with most, they can become dangerous. For example, the Ice Bucket Challenge, the Cinnamon Challenge, and the Skull Breaker. These were each an online phenomenon that were made popular thanks to Facebook, Instagram, and

Snapchat; however, while they were fun to watch, what we don't see is how much harm they were doing.

The Ice Bucket Challenge was a challenge that was meant to raise awareness for ALS. While the idea was there and some money was raised, all it did was push people to find unique and often crazy ways of doing the challenge.

Another challenge that I mentioned where herd mentality is not ideal is the Skull Breaker. This challenge is something that started off as a prank but has resulted in many teens around the world getting physically injured. Some even were injured so badly that there were permanent damages (Chiu, 2020).

These are just a few of the examples where the herd mentality and being a follower is not what you want.

Impact on Your Nervous System

Have you ever picked up your phone because you were sure it was vibrating? You saw the little green light flash and heard it vibrate across the table, only to pick it up and realize that your phone didn't go off. This is your nervous system being on hyper-alert. Your regular use of social media can trick your brain into believing you are getting notifications that aren't really there.

Reduced Attention Span

Scrolling through posts on social media can cause heavy users to have a diminished attention span. A news feed is made up of many short stories. You may even find yourself scrolling through so quickly that you don't have time to read a long story. Participating in this type of behavior frequently can stem into the rest of your life. Your brain can start to analyze things very quickly, becoming bored or distracted when they take too long. A reduced attention span like this can affect you at work, school, and even in your friendships.

Social media has been proven to cause significant issues in a person's mental health. Trying to keep up with the glorious lifestyles that fill up social media can be exhausting. It can also make you feel bad about yourself, as though your life is not as exciting or fulfilling as everyone else's.

The stress social media can create in people may lead to increased anxiety and even depression. In severe cases, it can even lead to suicidal thoughts. When social media has such a strong influence on a person's life, it can be very damaging.

Do You Really Have a Problem?

Whether you have a problem or not is a journey of self-discovery. Do any of the scenarios in this chapter sound like your life? Do you find yourself jealous of others or feeling like your life isn't good enough? Do you spend hours each night checking your newsfeeds and then feel fatigued the next day? Do you find you are often misunderstood on Twitter? Do you end up in back and forth arguments on social media? Any of these events may mean that you have a problem.

As you continue to read, you can learn more about what social media addiction and anxiety mean for your life. Chapters 6, 7, and 8 all have quizzes that you can take to understand better how social media is affecting your life. These quizzes are not intended to make you feel inadequate or self-conscious but help guide you on a path towards healing. Social media does not have to be a problem and does not have to control your life. Realizing this means you are well on your way to beating your addiction and overcoming your anxiety.

Remember, sometimes the first step is the hardest. Acknowledging and recognizing that we are online too much or that our relationships with friends and family are being affected is a massive step; therefore, you shouldn't discredit that. Something to consider though, is what happens when you don't want to change, when you don't want to get help, and when you allow yourself to be controlled by social media.

The goal of this chapter was to highlight the physical and psychological impacts social media has while also highlighting that there is a balance that can be had, and that is what's key. If anything, I hope that you will, in the next coming chapters, find that balance or solution you are looking for.

Chapter 5:

The Rise of Social Media and the Birth of Anxiety

"Social media has become a space in which we form and build relationships, shape self-identity, express ourselves, and learn about the world around us; it is intrinsically linked to mental health." - Shirley Cramer

Anxiety and social media seem to go hand in hand. Whether you suffer from a diagnosable case of anxiety or just experience pangs of it here and there, it is a feeling held by many. One would think that this means it is easier to discuss anxiety or that it would be prevalent; however, like with most mental health matters, there is a negative stigma associated with anxiety and what it looks like.

Anxiety can cause significant problems in your life, to the point that it bars you from engaging in enjoyable activities. It can be so intense that it controls your life. You do anything you can to avoid the overwhelming thoughts circling through your pain. While this is true of most forms of anxiety, it is also true for social media anxiety.

You may notice your anxiety from social media crops up in several ways. "Likes," and the feeling you get from receiving those "likes," can be a contributing factor to your stress. It may seem as though the more "likes" you get, the better you feel, but this is not necessarily true. Additionally, personal competition and envy can also cause a problem for you. They can make you want things you can't have, driving your mind mad with frustration. The same is true for shyness and the fear of missing out. Wanting a life that is not yours to have can create an internal struggle that manifests itself as anxiety.

Your anxiety from social media can be apparent in one or all of the above ways. When you read through, some explanations may sound exactly like you, while others seem far away. There is no one exact cause of social media anxiety, but rather a unique combination of events that make you feel that way.

It is essential to understand each factor because anxiety can cause social media addiction. In order to soothe your feelings, you turn to your socials because it feels better for the time being. Then, you inevitably run into the same experience that made you feel bad in the first place, so the cycle continues.

Finding what part of your social media experience triggers your anxiety is the key to overcoming it. When you know what drives the discomfort, you know what areas you need to combat. Notice the term is combat and not avoid.

Avoidance is not usually a technique for overcoming anxiety problems. In fact, entirely avoiding it can make the problem worse or even adopt a new form of anxiety. Instead, you should learn how to confront the problem head-on. Learning how to tolerate the feelings of discomfort and working through them will do you much more good than ignoring the problem entirely.

Quiz - Always, Sometimes, Never - How Anxious Are YOU?

Time for a break in reading and to check our anxiety levels when it comes to social media and our engagement on the various platforms. This quiz is not meant to be a definitive indicator of whether or not you suffer from anxiety or that your anxiety is a result of social media. This quiz is meant to be light-hearted and to be a means of opening up the lines of communication and understanding your own needs and expectations.

Remember, this quiz is not meant to indicate whether or not you have an addiction, or suffer from anxiety.

If you require more information on resources to help with your anxiety or social media usage, refer to **Chapter 10, Resources**.

Read the following statements, and write down whether it *always, sometimes,* or *never* applies to you.

1. I tend to dwell on situations that don't go as I planned or expected.
2. I can become fearful out of the blue.
3. When people get upset with me, I tend to find it hard to move on and dwell on it the rest of the day.
4. I have disturbing, upsetting, and/or repetitive dreams.
5. I struggle to move on from a problem.
6. I am easily alarmed or surprised.
7. I have trouble relaxing or being in the moment.
8. I sometimes spend hours upon hours trying to understand my feelings and reactions.
9. I dwell on things that I have not finished or things that I haven't accomplished.
10. I struggle falling or staying asleep.
11. I am sometimes not satisfied with the resolution to a problem and will dwell on it after the fact.
12. I am easily annoyed and frustrated.
13. I will go out of my way to avoid situations that make me uncomfortable or that could lead to a panic attack.
14. I will repeat a task over and over again until I feel that my fears, insecurities, or doubts are eased.
15. I worry about what people think of me.

Congratulations, that wasn't so bad now was it?

Before we discuss the results, remember, this quiz is not meant to tell you whether or not you suffer from anxiety or a social media addiction. This is merely meant to open the opportunity for discussion.

If you answered *"always"* to a majority of the preceding statements, this is an indication that you are more anxious than the average person. To be anxious means that you are highly concerned with others' perception of you, as well as what you put out there for others to see and possibly judge. When it comes to social media, someone who experiences emotions of anxiousness will find that they are drawn to positive engagement and reinforcement. This means that more often than not, a person will do whatever is necessary to meet the needs of these feelings.

For those who answered *"sometimes,"* this means that you have a moderate level of anxiousness. Most people experience a moderate level of anxiousness in their daily life. Some are a result of work, family, friends, and other forms of responsibility and expectation. Our levels of anxiousness can sometimes be heightened when we feel pressure or when we feel a need to be part of the in-crowd, our levels of anxiousness can go from moderate to severe.

Finally, if you responded *"never"* to a majority of these statements, it means that you have low levels of anxiousness or are not overly bothered by social media. This is a goal that many would like to achieve when it comes to social media or really anything of a similar nature. Low anxiousness often indicates a level of carefreeness that is not always experienced, yet it is what many strive for. Sometimes not caring about what people want or expect is the best way to live, and based on the statements, if you answered *never*, you probably let bygones be bygones.

Remember, these results are not definitive; they are not meant to diagnose you or any possible mental health issue. This quiz is meant to be a guide to help you have the foundation to begin the process of seeking help or assistance for your social media usage.

"Likes"

For many, the most critical factor of their social media is the "like" button. Instead of posting a truly accurate depiction of your life to your wall, it is plastered with the very best version of what you do. It shows how much 'fun' you had at the beach last week or your latest acquisition. Your posts talk about your upcoming vacation or your latest promotion. They show all of the very best aspects of your life, rather than an accurate reflection of what is going on.

Alternatively, you may post all of the worst parts of your life. Some people prefer to share their hardships because they seek sympathy from others. To be clear, everyone goes through hard times; posting about it can be therapeutic. But when you always post from a pessimistic, 'woe is me' place, you are likely doing so for attention. The purpose of both excessively happy and overly sad is the same; you are probably looking for attention.

The attention you look for comes in the form of "likes." The more "likes" you receive, the better you feel about yourself. The problem with this is that "likes," or lack thereof, can lead to anxiety and depression.

There are many negative things that can happen on social media, including bullying and trolling. However, one of the hardest ones to accept is not receiving enough "likes." This is because when you post a photo or comment, the goal is to receive a *"like."* When you don't get that, it can be crushing.

Not getting enough "likes" can make you feel as though you have inherent character flaws. It can make you feel as though you, as a person, are unlikable and need to make changes to be liked. That feeling can be carried from your online existence into your real world. You can develop social anxieties that make it challenging to manage your day-to-day life.

Social anxiety or phobia can make it hard for you to attend school or work. Even going to the grocery store can be difficult. You may feel as though you are being judged by every person you pass. It can feel like every person in the room is watching you intently, waiting to point and laugh.

Social anxieties are very challenging to live with. They tend to hold people back because they struggle to function in society. For example, someone with a social phobia may be afraid to eat in front of others. The anxiety and pressure they feel during that event may make them pass up social meals entirely. This can be a significant problem when you are trying to spend time with friends. Going out to eat or having dinner together is considered a normal thing to do with your peers. In fact, many cultures perceive sharing meal times together to be a core part of their traditions. Someone with a social phobia may choose to excuse themselves from experiences like this. When they skip out on these experiences, they miss out on important connections. The more they miss, the further apart they drift from their circle of friends, eventually becoming isolated.

In this example, the anxiety felt from not getting enough "likes" has a significant impact on their social life. The connection between social media and real-life is so closely connected that your "like" count can cause very serious, lasting problems.

Dopamine Hits

Receiving a "like" for one of your posts can boost your mood so instantaneously that it has been compared to receiving a hit of dopamine (Cristol, 2019). To fully comprehend what this parallel means, you must first understand what role dopamine plays for your brain and general well-being, as the hormones that our body releases play a significant role in our behaviors.

Dopamine is a chemical or neurotransmitter that is used to send messages throughout your nervous system. Dopamine is one of the ways that your brain and body connect when you feel pleasure. It also helps you focus, think, plan, find interests, and strive.

Much of your behavior, actions, and physicality are directly affected by the dopamine that runs through your body. Dopamine is at least partially responsible and linked to:

- Your ability to feel and stay motivated
- Controlling and responding to your heart rate
- Your ability to learn new concepts and skills
- The way your blood vessels function
- Your ability to get a good sleep or suffer from poor sleep
- Your mood stability
- Proper or irregular lactation
- Your attention span or lack thereof
- Your ability to move with ease or restriction
- Your vomiting reflex
- Your sensitivity to nausea
- How your brain processes pain

Dopamine exists naturally in your body, traveling along four pathways in your brain. Most people don't notice the effects of dopamine unless they experience some sort of problem with it. Like most other things, too much or too little dopamine can lead to various health problems.

Mental health disorders usually have more than one cause, but dopamine problems have been linked to mental health issues. Too much or too little can affect different parts of the brain. For example, schizophrenia can be related to having too much dopamine. Those who suffer from this may be subject to hallucinations and delusions. Interestingly, parts of the brain that don't get enough dopamine can lead to a lack of desire and motivation.

Other mental health issues such as addiction, have also been linked to dopamine. This is where the comparison of the feeling you get from receiving a "like" is most directly related. Some stimulant drugs give you a hit of dopamine as soon as you ingest it, sending messages of pleasure to your brain. The more you get, the more you want. As addiction progresses, you need more of the drug to get the same pleasure because your tolerance level builds. The same is true for "likes."

Your anxiety can build around the dopamine that hits your cravings. You may begin to feel anxious or withdrawn when you go long stretches without getting your "likes." Additionally, you can start to crave more "likes" for every post, taking on greater risk in your photos to get the reaction you are looking for. You may also find yourself posting more often to get your hit of dopamine more quickly.

Competing with Yourself

Competition in life can be a good thing. It can motivate self-improvement and inspire the desire to learn new things. However, too much competition can be dangerous, mainly when you compete with yourself.

Anxiety can build within when you feel like you must continuously compete with yourself (Hyatt, 2015). When it comes to social media, competition arises in terms of "likes," reactions, and reach. Socials provide users with a variety of statistics that tally how many followers you have, how many people "like" your posts, and how many people saw your post. Many businesses utilize these numbers to help grow their market, but you can be facing severe anxiety problems when you, as an individual, do it.

Your social media addiction can create anxiety when you analyze the numbers associated with your account. For example, one of the most popular numbers to look at is your follower count. This gives you an indication of how many people can see what you are posting. From here, you can analyze how many "likes" and reactions you get.

For many people, the goal is to have a high ratio of your followers "liking" your posts. If you feel not enough people are reacting, anxiety may set in. Why aren't you getting the reaction you want? Do you need to do something differently? Are you unlikable? Did you do something to make people angry? Do your followers find your content annoying? Questions like this can swirl through your brain, repeating themselves over and over. To alleviate that anxiety, you may try to get new followers or try adjusting your hashtags. With a more radical approach, you may begin taking photos that put you in a dangerous situation or reveal more of your body than you are comfortable with.

The problem continues to develop until you get to the point that you can no longer outdo yourself. Every time you post, you get the same reactions from the same people. No matter how impressive your photo is, you get the same number of likes. This state begins to weigh further on your anxiety. You may incessantly check your wall to see how many people have "liked" it, refreshing your page over and over, hoping for a different result. Behavior like this is damaging to your self-esteem.

Your anxiety can then continue into your real life. You may think you have turned into a boring person that no one wants to spend time with or get to know better. After all, if people don't "like" your posts online, why would they like you in person? This could not be less true, though your internal competition factor makes you feel so bad about yourself that you think it is.

Personal competition and anxiety can be a dangerous combination. Understanding that not all posts are going to garner the same reaction is essential for your well-being. There is enough competition in the world; you do not need to put yourself through the turmoil of trying to one-up yourself.

Envy

Envy is an emotion that is often conveyed in many pieces of great literature, but it is also an emotion that is frequently associated with social media.

Look at the following quotes:

"The jealous are troublesome to others, but a torment to themselves." - William Penn

"Never underestimate the power of jealousy and the power of envy to destroy. Never underestimate that." - Oliver Stone

Envy is one of the most dangerous afflictions to come with social media addiction and anxiety. Everyone feels envious from time to time, but socials can suck you into a trap, making you think that everyone else's life is so much better than yours. It can make you feel like your life is boring or has very little meaning.

Jealousy can feel like real, physical pain. When you feel envious or jealous, you may begin to feel a sense of nausea in the pit of your stomach. You may feel a tingling sensation in your arms and legs. Your eyes may even begin to dilate. All of your senses are heightened, your ears perked, and your vision clear. This is your body's flight or fight response kicking in. Your body is reacting to the threat registered in your brain, making it ready to act accordingly.

That fight or flight response can be particularly dangerous with social media. It can make you react at the moment with actions you can come to regret. Later on, when you take a step back, you can see that there was probably a different way to handle the situation.

The first way you may find yourself in trouble with envy on social media is by wanting what someone else has. Maybe it is a car, a new house, a vacation, or even hanging out with the 'cool group' at school. In order to make those things happen, you may spend money you don't have or take time off from work you can't afford. To hang out with the 'coolest kids in school,' you may find yourself engaging in behavior you aren't comfortable with.

Once you have made these decisions, you will see that the outcome may not be what you hoped. You may be house poor, working to pay off your mortgage with nothing left over for fun. Or, you may be denied for a car loan, making you feel worse about yourself. Maybe your real friends found out what you did with the 'cool kids' and are now mad at you. All of these scenarios could have been prevented had you let the envy go. Instead, the anxiety took over, and you ended up worse off than you were before.

There is another way that envy on social media can cause significant problems. It comes with following or stalking an ex on your socials. Break-ups hurt; that is a fact of life. To make it even more painful, social media gives you the ability to see exactly what your ex is up to. You get to see their new and improved hairstyle, the new special person in their life, and how well they seem to be doing without you. Seeing posts like that are incredibly painful and can make you do foolish things.

Envy of your ex's new life can make you do things like post threatening messages on their new partner's wall or sending numerous messages declaring your undying love. Had you not seen their wall, would you have ever behaved that way? Most people would say not. Being exposed to the uncomfortable imagery makes you do things you normally would avoid.

That is the power of envy and anxiety of social media; it fuels our constant desire to have more and be better, rather than to be content and give back.

Status by Means of Ranking

In the same way that you can compete with yourself on social media, you can compete with others. All of the numbers associated with social platforms mean you have a direct comparison method to see how you stack up against your friends and frenemies.

A number is a black and white scale that shows you exactly where you stand. It shows you how 'popular' you are versus someone else. If your friends have way more followers than you, it can bring on an anxious feeling, making you think you aren't likable. If their posts garner more attention, it can hurt your feelings. Both of these scenarios can affect your self-esteem.

Those numbers can also make others treat you differently because they feel empowered. A high follower or reaction count can go to a person's head, making them feel more important. In turn, they treat you poorly, or lesser than, and act as though they are superior to you. Being treated poorly can affect your self-esteem, making you believe what they say to be true.

Status ranking on social media is a dangerous tool that feeds into your real life. When you accept the numbers to be representative of your worth, your internal value will fluctuate along with them. Every time you get a good result, you feel good about yourself. Every time you get a poor one, you feel bad. It is a vicious cycle that follows you everywhere you go. Learning to separate the physical numbers from your self-worth is essential to avoiding increased social media anxiety.

It is essential to understand that numbers do not tell the whole story. When you look at your friend count, how many people are you really friends with? Does the number reflect people you care about or just people you have come across in life? The quality of your friends list should matter more than the quantity (Eisenberger & Lieberman, 2005).

The same is true about your "like" count. Are strangers the ones "liking" your posts, or is it your real friends? If you have fewer "likes," but they are all by people who care about your well-being, you are better off. Keep in mind that when people have a significant number of followers, it is likely that they don't know them all on a personal level. They may "friend" people to increase their count for the sole purpose of seeming more popular than they are.

Neither of these scenarios is easy to come by mentally. It is easy to compare yourself to others, thinking that you rank below them because your number counts are lower. Instead of falling into that anxiety trap, learn to appreciate your followers' quality rather than the number.

Diminishing Impulse Control

As we have discussed, so much of social media addiction and anxiety is directly related to "likes" and follower reactions. Everyone requires attention; it is a basic human need. Socializing with others is linked to your happiness and contentment in life. So when you aren't getting the attention you desire from social media in the form of likes and comments, you act out in an attempt to be seen.

When you feel a rush of intense emotion, you need to do something with it. Social media can be an excellent outlet for that type of energy. However, it can also lead to some problems. Thinking before you act has long been an issue for many people. When you make a quick emotional choice rather than a well-thought-out response, problems may arise. When you spend a lot of your time on social media, those impulse controls can be further affected, resulting in knee-jerk reactions to an event in your life.

Acting without restraint can come into play when you do not get enough attention. When this happens, your anxiety is triggered. To relieve that anxiety, many people spend more time on social media. You know that you can get the attention you so desire with a properly worded post or flirty picture. Even though you know that social media is where you lack the attention, you turn to it because you know it worked at one point. It is similar to a child acting out for attention from their parents. They know that when they act out with bad behavior, their parents will give them their attention. A child craving attention would prefer even negative attention rather than none at all.

Look back at the posts you have made. Were any of those done as a result of looking for attention? Do you have any photos that make you uncomfortable to look at? Did you share information outside of your typical character? Then analyze how it made you feel after. Did it make you feel better in the moment but worse later on? Was there any fallout like a fight with friends or a partner? Those are examples of times you used social media without restraint. Those are the times that any attention was better than none. But looking back, was it really? This is one of the dangers of diminished impulse control that social media can create.

Your diminishing impulse control can be problematic in another way. The problem can lie with your impulse to check your social walls. Every time you pull out your phone, you probably scroll through your apps to see what is happening in the online world. Even if you tell yourself not to, you struggle to put your phone away without checking.

For anyone trying to get over a social media addiction, this may be the biggest struggle. Your phone is just sitting there in your pocket, waiting to be opened. When you go to send a text, you have an overwhelming desire to click on that app. The anxiety is burning inside you, telling you that something is going on, and you need to check it out. That anxiety is likely soothed when you give in and see that you have not missed anything. Everything is just the same as when you left it a few minutes ago. But at least you feel better to know that for sure.

That lack of impulse control is also what makes you check your phone at inappropriate times. Even just seeing your phone on the table can get your mind buzzing. That is why you feel the need to check it when you are sitting at the dinner table with your family, in the middle of the workday, or while hanging out with friends. Your bad habit may bother everyone around you, but the anxiety nags so hard that you do anything you can to relieve it.

You may find yourself in trouble at work, school, or even home as a result of your poor impulse control. Learning to overcome that anxiety and regain your impulse control can help you move forward to overcoming your addiction to social media.

Social Anxiety and Shyness

Social media and social anxiety are complex subjects. While it can be surmised that online socials can help people overcome some shyness, it can also be a problem, making people who are already shy struggle even more. Additionally, someone who was once happy to be on social media can be scared by what they feel is negative attention. This can cause them to develop social anxiety in both their real and online life.

If you are shy, social media can cause further problems for several reasons. The first is, many sites like Snapchat or Facebook are initially set up by creating a friends list of people you already know. If you are shy, you may not have many, or any, friends to add. That makes it very difficult for you to break out of your shyness.

Further, when you make many friends online, those friendships may exist only in that universe. You may know them through your phone, and that is it. While it may be better than no connection at all, it can leave you feeling unfulfilled in the friendship department. This is especially true if you never meet them in person or if they refuse to meet in person.

Alternatively, you may be shy in person but very comfortable online. Because you are so dynamic online, it may stop you from feeling the need to socialize with people in person. This further develops your outside shyness. This can cause you problems in the workplace and at school because you still feel very socially uncomfortable.

Social anxiety is a diagnosable mental health issue that can be exacerbated by the use of social media. It can be similar to shyness, except that it is usually more intense. It can stop a person in their tracks, making them so uncomfortable in social situations that they do everything they can to avoid them.

If you have social anxiety, you may also be depressed. If that's the case, you may find yourself posting things that others do not find appealing. Your way of expressing yourself can be challenging for others to relate to, so they don't respond well to your posts. They may ignore the posts entirely or make unhelpful comments. The underwhelming reaction can be hurtful, making you feel even more uncomfortable in social situations.

Social media sites can also be hard on people with social anxiety because of the comparison factor. When you scroll through your news feed, it's filled with people who have all those things you want in life. Whether it is a family or your dream job, you see what you don't have. It's hard to see this because you may feel that you cannot relate to others. It can also make you feel worse about your own life, furthering your desire to avoid social situations.

There is another issue that those with social anxiety may face. Social media can give lots of background information about a person, almost too much. If you are meeting someone new, you may try to prepare by learning all you can about them. Feeling like you know them ahead of time may make you feel more comfortable. However, once you finally meet them, they may feel uncomfortable about how much you know. This can lead to an awkward encounter, making for more social discomfort.

Social media can be both wonderful and detrimental for shy or socially anxious people. It creates a controlled environment, making it easier for you to interact with others. There is more opportunity for you to link up with people who share similar interests. Plus, since you are talking from behind a screen, you have a little more time to plan out what you are going to say.

If you suffer from social media anxiety, however, you may be more likely to have a social media addiction. Finding the balance in the middle is vital. Otherwise, it can lead to a worsened case of anxiety or an addiction to social media.

FOMO

Fear of missing out, or FOMO, is a real thing. The colloquial term has been adopted by many social media users and gets thrown around in everyday conversations (Penenberg, 2010). However, FOMO can be a significant anxiety-causing problem.

Fear of missing out makes a person feel as though there is something going on that they are not a part of. The feeling can consume you, causing severe bouts of anxiety. To soothe the discomfort, you check out social media over and over again to make sure nothing is going on without you.

The pain of thinking that your peers are doing something, know something, or have something you don't, comes from a place of unhappiness. If you are not satisfied with your life the way it is, you may be subject to FOMO. It may also be one of the reasons you suffer from social media addiction.

People who fear that something is going on without them may find themselves unable to sleep at night until they have checked through all of their social accounts. They need to know that nothing is going on without them. Unfortunately, checking their socials pacifies the feelings for only a short period of time. While trying to fall asleep, they may feel the pressure to check again, just to be absolutely sure. When they wake up, the first thing they do is check through their socials, only to be sure everything was how they left it.

Fear of missing out can cause serious problems with your mental health. It can cause mood swings, social anxiety, loneliness, low self-esteem, and a feeling of inferiority. A big problem here is that those with FOMO turn to social media to relieve the feeling, but social media caused it in the first place.

If you intensely suffer from FOMO, you may notice that you suffer in other areas of your life as well. Socially, your friends or family may be bothered with your constant need to check your phone. You may get easily distracted by your phone at work, causing trouble with your boss and coworkers. You may even feel such strong urges to check your socials that you pick up your phone while driving. This is a dangerous behavior that could make you cause a serious accident.

While FOMO is thrown around as a conversational word, it can be a real problem for people (Robinson & Smith, 2020). If you have it, the issue should not be taken lightly. Working towards overcoming your social media addiction may be essential to dealing with this form of anxiety.

Anxiety and Social Media

Evidently, there are many ways that your social media obsession can be causing anxiety. Not having enough likes or reactions to your posts and photos causes not only anxiety but self-esteem issues. Waiting and wondering why you aren't getting the comments you desire can cause you serious internal pain. You may feel worse about yourself than you did before posting. You may also find yourself posting inappropriate things in order to drive more likes.

Additionally, things like envy and self-comparison drive you to engage in questionable behavior. You may spend money you don't have to buy an item you really don't need. Alternatively, you may become friends with people you can't trust just to appear more likable.

Interestingly, both of these are age-old problems that have existed for years. Think of your years in high school where you do whatever you had to in order to fit in. For many people, once they left high school, those feelings were gone. However, social media can make those feelings resurface, regardless of age. Just as in high school, you look for ways to cope with those overwhelming anxieties. Understand that whatever you have been doing to soothe the anxiety probably does not do you much good in the long run. This is because pacifying a stressor does not solve the problem permanently. Instead, it only allows you to deal with it at the moment.

No matter what exact symptom is linked to your anxiety, you probably feel uncomfortable most of the time. Second-guessing yourself or feeling like you aren't good enough is a challenging mental state of mind. One of the best ways to alleviate that is to work on your anxiety or addiction. Overcoming it can bring you a sense of peace and happiness in your world, just the way it is. As you read on, pay specific attention to Chapter 8, where you can learn helpful ways to deal with your anxiety or addiction.

Chapter 6:

Selfie-Esteem

"Social media websites are no longer performing an envisaged function of creating a positive communication link among friends, family and professionals. It is a veritable battleground, where insults fly from the human quiver, damaging lives, destroying self-esteem and a person's sense of self-worth" - Anthony Carmona

Selfies are one of the most popular styles of photos to appear on social media. They are so common that the word selfie was added to the Oxford Dictionary in 2013. Before that, it wasn't even considered a real word. Their popularity blew up, and suddenly most social media news feeds featured up close and personal images of your friends.

At one point, selfies may have been considered harmless. It was a handy way to take a picture when there was no one around to hold the camera. Over the years, they have become a phenomenon from which emerged concerning trends. Selfies are now linked to negative concepts such as lower self-esteem or an inflated sense of self.

Selfies can impact you and your social media addiction in a wide variety of ways. It is essential to fully comprehend each factor so you can understand the effect they have on your life. Otherwise, you may think that your anxiety or addiction has nothing to do with selfies, when in fact, they may be directly tied to this style of photo. They can have a much more significant impact than people realize.

Quiz — Are You a Selfie Fanatic?

Do you want to see how much you *care* for that perfect selfie?

Take this quick quiz to see whether or not that perfect shot not only matters but exists in your eyes.

While you take this quick quiz, it is important to note that this is not meant to make you feel as though you should be ashamed, nor should you take this to mean anything major or significant.

This quiz is meant to help you see just how far you are willing to push the boundaries for the perfect shot. It is also meant to open the lines of communication and self-awareness when it comes to our perception of self.

Now, sit back, breathe and relax. While some tests are about a pass or fail, this test is about personal growth and development!

Answer yes or no to the following statements and then tally up your responses.

1. I can't take a picture without touching up my makeup, or making sure that I'm in an outfit that no one has seen.
2. I always check the photo after it has been taken, and then I take a few more to make sure that all angles and sides of me are taken so I can pick the best one to share.
3. "Out of Bounds" is not enough to stop me from getting the perfect shot at major attractions.
4. When I wake up I take a selfie and will share it on my Snapchat or social media account - but not before I put on makeup or freshen up.
5. I get upset when no one talks about my selfie or notices the effort I put into looking good, even though I don't want them to think I put any effort in.

6. I have lost friendships and relationships because I took too many selfies.
7. I have gotten in trouble for breaking or bending the rules to get the perfect selfie.
8. Sharing my selfies makes me feel like a celebrity and an influencer.
9. If I don't take a selfie at least 4-5 times a day, I feel I need to make up for lost photos and time.
10. I have pretended to take a selfie that looks as though someone else is taking the photo, but in reality, I took it myself.

Congratulations, you have finished the Selfie Quiz!

Now, it may not be easy to look at your responses, but what did you answer? Did you have more "yes" than "no"?

If you said "yes" to more than half the statements, it could mean that you are heavily motivated and controlled by taking a selfie. Moments may happen with friends and family, but it is more important that you capture that perfect shot.

For those who answered "yes" to most of the responses, this can be a sign that you need to reevaluate your "selfie game" as it is most likely affecting your relationships, or it is going to affect your relationships.

On the other hand, if you answered "no" to most of the responses, you have a good balance between when to take a selfie and share, and when to just savor the moment. If you are able to answer "no" to most if not all the preceding questions, you are aware of the potential impact that too much selfie-taking can have on your relationships and also your well-being. It could also indicate that you do not require reinforcement and validation the same way that someone who posts constantly does.

Impact of Constant Self-Interactions

Selfies are a self-interaction. They are taken by you and assessed by you. It is somewhat like staring in a mirror for hours on end. Doing it too much can cause you to behave in ways that are outside of your real personality. Instead, you begin to act like the person you want to be.

Interacting with yourself too much can make you judge yourself too harshly. You may find what you think are flaws, and you now work hard to cover them up. For example, if your hair does a 'weird' wave in every selfie, you may begin to be self-conscious about it. When you are out and about, you may continuously try and flatten out your hair. You obsess over it, thinking about it every few minutes, wondering who else notices it. If you had never spent so much time looking at your face in selfies, would you have ever noticed it?

Taking selfies in public also poses another problem. Instead of experiencing the world around you, you spend your time taking a picture of yourself. You end up missing out on what is happening around you. When you get home and see your pictures, do you remember the fantastic landscape in the background, or do you analyze how you look in the photo?

The constant self-interactions brought on by selfies may make you prioritize your looks over everything else. It may feel like the only thing you have to offer the world is your good looks. However, your looks are likely the least important part of your day. Your sharp mind, your snappy humor, and unique point of view are your most endearing qualities. When you focus too much on your looks, these things come second. You can lose sight of how dynamic you are when you spend too much time analyzing your photos.

Distorted View of Self

Expert selfie-takers know that there is a science behind the perfect selfie. It is not a matter of simply holding up your phone, pointing and shooting. In fact, the perfect selfie (Ward et al., 2018) requires a combination of the following:

1. You must be far enough away from the camera, ideally 5 feet.
2. You must have adequate lighting.
3. You need to avoid having shadows splashed across your face.
4. You need to know when to use your flash.
5. You must know your best features and then highlight them.
6. You must know and use the best angles for your facial features.
7. You need to smile as though you are having the time of your life.
8. You need to use the RIGHT filters and apps.
9. You must take lots of selfies to get the best shot.
10. You cannot over-edit.

Selfies are made to look as though they quickly capture a natural moment in time. When you look through this list, it is obvious that they are anything but natural.

The problem is that when you don't achieve that perfect shot, you may develop a distorted view of your face. You may judge your nose or lips too harshly. You may think that your cheeks look fat or your eyebrows are too thin. Your distorted view usually coincides with your biggest insecurity.

The interesting takeaway is this: the distortion you perceive may actually be because you haven't taken the selfie following the proper recipe. When you take the photo too close, your nose often appears much larger than it is. And no matter how many times you take that photo, the result is still the same. You could combine steps 2-10 in the above list, but your nose will always look more prominent if you are too close. However, how are you ever supposed to take a selfie from 5 feet away? The standards are nearly impossible to achieve, meaning you will almost always have a distorted view of your face.

Plastic Surgeries

The distortion a selfie provides can lead you to take drastic measures. If your nose looks too big or your lips look too thin in every photo, you may decide enough is enough; it's time to do something about it. The only way to change such permanent facial features is with plastic surgery.

Plastic surgery is not always a negative thing. It can be quite helpful in some aspects. However, it is problematic if you decide to go under the knife because of your selfies. Since you are likely not following the perfect recipe for your selfie, you probably aren't looking at an accurate depiction of your face. Meaning you are making drastic changes to your appearance unnecessarily.

Plastic surgery used to be only for celebrities, but now cosmetic surgery is available for anyone who can afford it. It is often thought of as a simple surgery because it seems like such a routine thing. However, it is a very serious procedure that takes months to heal from. Many complications can arise from cosmetic procedures; some that don't appear for several years. It should not be entered into lightly, yet it seems like a quick and easy solution. Plastic surgery also costs thousands of dollars; some people even go into significant debt to pay for it. Plastic surgery is anything but simple and often cannot solve your problems the way you think it will.

To further complicate the matter, if you do engage in some sort of surgery, you will likely be pleased every time you take a selfie. The perceived problem is fixed because your nose is the perfect size and shape. However, what happens when you are in a traditional photo where someone stands far away to get the shot? Are you still happy with your augmentation, or is your nose too small and your lips too full? That is the trouble with undergoing surgery just because of what you see in a selfie. Your view is distorted, and therefore, so is your perception of your face.

Oversharing

An effective social media wall is a balance of sharing personal information while withholding some of your thoughts and photos. Though the purpose of your wall is to share your life, there is a point where oversharing can be an issue. This tends to be a big problem with selfies.

When you get used to posting selfies all the time, you may become numb to the content. You are so accustomed to sharing your life through these photos that you stop assessing the content to see if it is appropriate. People on your feed may be uncomfortable seeing the image or may think it is distasteful. While you may feel 'if you don't like it, don't look at it' or 'it's my wall, and I will post what I want,' remember that your social media is a reflection of you as a person. Many people, such as future employers and parents, can see what you are sharing.

Oversharing can come in several forms. The first is by showing your body. Having the self-confidence to post revealing photos of yourself may help you have a positive body image and boost your self-esteem (Sigala, 2018). However, it can also lead to posting provocative photos of yourself. Ones that you may regret in later years or that you don't want just anyone to see. The problem with social media is that even if you have privacy settings, most images can be found with a little detective work.

Oversharing can also come in the form of too much information, or TMI, as it is commonly known. Some details of your life are better kept to conversations between you and your close friends and family. All of your contacts do not need to know about your latest sexual conquest or intimate details of your latest doctor's appointment. And yet, some users do feel okay sharing these things through their selfies and timeline. This activity can cause others to see you in a different light, affecting your in-person interactions as well as your online ones.

Impact on Self-Esteem

Your selfies can have a direct impact on your self-esteem. Since they often show off your face, body, or style, the reaction you receive can make you feel either pleased or sad. That feeling can then carry into your daily life, affecting your self-esteem. If you tend to feel bad after posting your selfie, you may end up suffering from low self-esteem. By contrast, if the reactions are superb, you may end up with an over-inflated concept of yourself.

Low

Generally, only your very best selfies are posted online. But to get to that point, you probably took dozens of shots. When you look through the photos afterward, it is likely that you carefully analyzed each one, nit-picking on every single detail of your face. While you may feel satisfied with the best photo, you still went through the process of tearing yourself down. If you pay attention to the voice in your head, it is probably very negative; reminding you about what you perceive to be your worst asset. This can lead to even greater self-consciousness and more frequent negative self-talk.

While you may be happy with the one shot you post, you still have all of the 'bad' ones that didn't make the cut. The rest of them are housed in the pictures folder on your phone. Do you delete these as soon as you are done? Probably not. Many people keep them on their phones. What do you do with those photos? It is likely that you skim through from time to time, reassessing the images all over again. You may browse through, thinking some of the shots are better than you remember. But, upon closer examination, you find the flaws all over again. This is very dangerous to your self-esteem. It is yet another way you tear yourself down, allowing the voice in your head to stew negative thoughts.

Selfies can also cause low self-esteem based on the reaction they receive from your friends and followers. It can be exceedingly hurtful not to get the positive reinforcement you were hoping for. You may feel ugly, unworthy, or lonely. Though you may be lonely, you are neither ugly nor unworthy. Unfortunately, it is so difficult to push those thoughts out of your mind. That negative self-talk can reappear every time you post a new photo or look back through your wall. It can even seep into your everyday life, further impacting your self-esteem.

Grandiose

The opposite is also true about selfies. They can give you a grandiose or an overinflated sense of self. When you begin to receive a flood of positive feedback, it may make you think you are better than others. Having this mentality is a problem for both you and the people in your life.

Having inflated self-esteem can make you feel entitled, causing you to have unrealistic expectations or make unfair demands. You may think that you deserve special treatment for merely showing up. You may think that others are lucky even to be able to speak with you. This kind of behavior is more than likely unwarranted and makes others dislike being in your company.

At its most extreme, grandiose self-esteem can mean you have a narcissistic personality disorder. Narcissists struggle to empathize with others because their sense of self-importance is too high. They tend to need excessive amounts of admiration and attention. A narcissist believes that their needs are so much more important than others, treating them poorly in order to get what they want. They also tend to be very good at manipulation, making it difficult to establish healthy relationships.

Interestingly, some people with an outwardly inflated self-esteem actually suffer from low self-esteem. Their portrayal of self-confidence is a way to cope with their true feelings about themselves.

Trouble with Relationships

Posting too many selfies can lead to trouble in relationships. Though you may think it is a personal picture and only affects you, this is not necessarily true. It can affect the person you are in a relationship with, your future relationships, and even your future employment.

If you are in a relationship, your partner may struggle with the content of your selfies. They may feel you are sharing too much of your body or too much of your life together. It is natural to feel like you want to keep some details of your relationship private. When you share too much online, it can make your partner feel vulnerable or frustrated, leading to fighting and disagreements.

If you aren't in a relationship, sharing too many selfies can make you appear to be inauthentic. Others may think you are fake, judging you without really knowing you. Even though you are a good person with a dynamic personality, they may judge you based on your photos and assume you are unapproachable. You can miss out on great relationships because people believe you think you are too good for them.

Additionally, people may treat you more harshly and make inappropriate comments on your social walls. When you post a photo online, many people think that they have free reign of what they can say. Etiquette goes out of the window. Opening yourself up to those kinds of comments can make it difficult for you to build relationships with others. People may not want to get to know you, or partners may find it challenging to come to your defense over and over again.

Selfies can also affect your professional relationships. Many current and future employers look through a person's social media accounts to see what their online presence looks like. If you have too many selfies, especially provocative ones, an employer may be less likely to hire you. Since you represent the company, they don't want to employ someone who seems to have a bad reputation.

Anxious Feelings

If you suffer from social media anxiety, selfies may be one of your most significant stressors. Selfies mark a vulnerable moment for many people. It is hard to feel that your photo looks as good as all the others circling through your newsfeed. It is even harder to know that your post is going to be judged by every one of your social media contacts.

The feeling of anxiety probably begins with setting up the shot. Your phone may be riddled with a series of takes, all in an attempt to get a good photo. You may have changed the angle numerous times, tried turning around to find better light, flipped your hair, and changed your face. In the end, you may not even have posted any photos because you were so disappointed in them. You may feel as though you are the only one who struggles so badly to find that perfect shot. Realizing that even professionals need to take multiple takes to find a great picture does not help you feel any better. All you feel is an overwhelming amount of stress and disappointment.

The next piece of anxiety may come from how many likes your post receives. Likes tend to feel like a measure of accomplishment or acceptance -the more people who like your photo, the better looking you are. It is normal to feel good or bad based on the number of likes, even though that is not necessarily a healthy reaction. Your self worth should not be tied to how many people react to your selfie, and yet it happens all the time. Your anxiety can creep up as you wait for your first likes and then again to see how many you get overall.

For many, the anxiety continues in the comments section of your post. Are people saying nice things? Are they reacting the way you hope? Did someone make a comment that tears you down? Did they make an unkind joke? Getting a notification that a comment was made can be thrilling and nerve-racking at the same time. If a comment is terrible, it can be hard to recover emotionally, driving you further down the road of social media anxiety.

Unfortunately, you may also experience another moment of anxiety. This comes from who did or didn't react to your photo. When someone you expected to say something nice didn't, it can cause you to have hurt feelings. Then, you may wonder if you did something wrong, making you worry even more. Alternatively, you may experience anxiety when someone you didn't expect to like your photo does. You may wonder what it means - are they interested in you? Was it a mistake? Were they just being nice? All of this is overwhelming.

Anxiety is prevalent in the world of selfies. The entire experience can be so nerve-racking that you choose to forgo these types of photos entirely. Or you may still post them and stew in your anxiety, waiting to breathe a breath of fresh air once you get the reaction you hoped. Either way, selfies can cause harmful feelings of anxiety.

Seeking Perfection

When you look through your phone, are most of your photos taken in the selfie-style? And how many of those did you get perfect on the first try? It's likely that you spent quite a bit of time taking several attempts to get the right one.

This is striving for perfection in your photos. The problem here is that perfection does not exist. Taking photos over and over again is not a realistic depiction of yourself or your life. This is especially true if you add filters.

This is not to say that all filters are bad. Some are fun, such as the dog filter or holiday filters, but filters that smooth your skin, tone your muscles, or round out your curves, are artificial representations of the way you look. Having the ability to alter your appearance in photos can make it so that you refuse to post honest pictures of yourself. You may feel embarrassed or self-conscious because you don't want to look anything other than your best.

At its outset, social media may have better represented true life. However, it has long since molded into illusions. Perfection is only in touched-up photos, but you may find yourself aiming for it anyway. With this, you can adopt the mindset that you look bad when you are your natural, unfiltered self.

Comparing Yourself to Others

When you take and post selfies, you may be doing so while comparing yourself to others. Whether you realize it or not, you probably judge how you look in comparison to others in their selfies. Do your lips look as full? Are your muscles as defined? How does your outfit make you look? You are always thinking about how you stack up against others. This can make you feel self-conscious or unhappy with your life.

Another way you compare yourself is by the number of online responses your photos and posts receive. Did you get as many likes and reactions as your friends? Did the same people like your photo? Or did you neglect to acquire a response from the person you wanted, even though they liked your friend's post? All of this comparison can be exhausting and bad for your well-being.

When you use social media to compare yourself to others, you decrease your personal value level. You also may begin to compare yourself more outside of social media. The behavior and feelings can seep into your real life as well as your online one. When that starts to happen, you can experience damaging feelings and thoughts about yourself.

You may not realize this is happening to you. It can be a slow start that becomes more accelerated over time. Sit and listen to your thoughts when you take a selfie. What does your self-talk sound like? Is it harmful, telling you that you should have a slimmer waist or fuller lips? Do you feel confident about that photo, or do you feel bad about yourself? If your responses to this are mostly negative, you will likely compare yourself to others too harshly and too frequently.

Sometimes, however, comparing yourself to others can help motivate you to make positive changes. For example, if you tend to eat unhealthy foods, you may be inspired to make a change. This transition is good for you both inside and out. Your physical well-being is an essential factor in your life. Eating poorly can lead to obesity, health complications, and even premature death. If your desire to take better selfies leads you to undergo a positive lifestyle change, then that could be a good thing.

Selfie Addiction

If your addiction to social media is taking over your life, you may be surprised to learn that the dependency can be even more profound. Selfies can actually be an addiction in and amongst themselves. Many people assume that the craving is related to your entire online persona, but for some, it can be just this one type of photo that has them hooked.

If you measure your self-worth based on your "likes," you can become dependent on posting selfies. When you feel sad and are in need of a pick-me-up, you may post a selfie. When you are dressed up and looking good, you post a selfie to further that validation. No matter your feeling, you turn to a selfie to get the reaction you desire. You may feel desperate for the attention you receive, making you crave it. Some people have related "likes" to a drug; the more you get, the more you want. One of the fastest ways to get those "likes" is with a stunning selfie.

The most unfortunate part of this addiction is that posting too many selfies can make you unlikable. Lots of people dislike it when their friends' news feed is loaded with selfies. Users who do this can be seen as annoying, less relatable, and less likable. However, you may never know this because your friends give you positive reactions to your photos anyway. So, secretly they are annoyed by you but won't tell you, though they may begin to treat you differently. If you notice your relationship with them changing, but you don't know why, it may be directly related to your selfies. Though this example is extreme, it shows the impact a selfie addiction can have on your life.

An addiction is a very complex part of the problems associated with selfies. If you are unsure whether you are addicted to selfie-taking, don't post one next time you want to; resist the urge. See how you feel afterward. If you can't do it or breathe a sigh of relief when you finally do, you may have aselfie addiction.

Selfies Aren't All Bad

While selfies can get a bad rap, they can also have a useful role in society. When you post a selfie, it shows that you have enough self-confidence to be vulnerable. Self-confidence is one of the most critical factors in your psychological well-being. A selfie can reinforce that and even improve it.

Also, selfies do not necessarily have to be posted as a way to show off your body or made-up face. Instead, they can be posted to share how you are spending your time. For example, you may enjoy taking selfies at your soccer game, showing your teammates running in the background. If the purpose of posting the photo was to document a time in your life, then the picture is a lovely addition to your wall.

Additionally, selfies can be a positive post when they depict a genuine friend or family moment. Spending time with people you love and support is an important facet of your life. Documenting your time together with a selfie should not be seen as a negative. Instead, it is a moment that you and your loved ones can remember fondly.

Selfies can also help play a role in communication with others. When you include another person, or persons, in your photo, they often want a copy. It can be a great way to stay in contact, inspire a more profound friendship, or even get someone's phone number. Photos get people talking, especially ones that they are included in.

Pictures of other people can be shared at any time, too. So, if you find yourself having gone a long stretch without talking to a friend, sending them a selfie of yourselves can reignite that relationship. Selfies make for a fun walk down memory lane.

Remembering that selfies have their place in social media is an important thought. Thinking that all of your selfies are inappropriate or self-indulgent can cause you to fall further into an anxious state. Rather, know that selfies can be fantastic documentation of a special moment in your life.

The Balancing Act of the Selfie

Recognizing that selfies can be both good and bad is essential. The good news is that you do not have to avoid having selfies on your profile. Selfie-lovers can let out a sigh of relief. However, understanding when and where to use the selfie is the key.

So, when is it okay to post a selfie? Selfies are great to show your online following special moments in your life. They are excellent for gathering all your friends to squeeze into a frame. They are a fun way to take a photo of you meeting a celebrity. They can even be great for showing off all your hard work in the gym. Selfies work well when the goal is to share your life.

But then, when is it wrong to post a selfie? There is no black and white answer here. It is more about moderation. Try to avoid posting too many selfies. Even if you get great reactions from them, overall, it does more harm than good. Every image on your wall should not be a selfie, especially ones that appear to be very similar.

Also, consider how a selfie makes you feel. Do you feel anxious waiting for those "likes?" When you get a "like," do you feel better about yourself? What happens when you don't get those "likes?" Selfies can be directly associated with your self-worth. If you only feel good about yourself when you get many good comments from people, you are probably too dependent on selfies.

The best way to manage your selfie posting is with balance. If you want to post one, be sure to follow it up with something different in your next post. Your wall should show your dynamic personality, not just one side of it. Selfies absolutely have a place in social media. They are not all bad and do not need to be avoided at all costs.

Going forward, be aware of how often you post and how it makes you feel. Finding new ways to express yourself can be both exciting and liberating.

Chapter 7:

Addiction — The Impact

"Recovery is an ongoing process, for both the addict and his or her family. In recovery there is hope. And hope is a wonderful thing." - Dean Dauphinais

Fully understanding your addiction means realizing how it is impacting your life. You may have noticed that your time spent on social media takes up too much time in your life or makes you have negative thoughts. These are common associations with social media addiction, but the actual impact can be much more significant.

There are areas of your life that are affected that may be surprising to you. For example, social media addiction can lead to eating disorders and financial stress. Afflictions like this are more common than you might realize, and you may even be suffering from one or more without knowing it.

Read through this chapter to understand the areas of your life that may be impacted by your addiction. This helps to give you a clear view of what is really happening in your world. Remember that the goal of this book is to help you overcome your addiction and anxiety. That means you may have to face some unpleasant facts. Do your best to avoid negative self-talk.

Acknowledging the issues socials have caused does not mean you need to feel bad about yourself. Instead, take in the information and move forward, being more conscientious of your actions.

One of the best ways to assess how and if your life is being affected by social media is by taking this quiz. This quiz can give you a better understanding of your well-being in relation to your socials.

Quiz - What's Your Social Media Style?

Do you know how much time you spend browsing through your social media platform?

Do you put your phone down and wonder where all the time has gone?

Do you find your neck hurting, or are you hunching over more than usual?

Take the following quiz and see what your social media style is.

Remember that sometimes we may not want to be honest with ourselves, but this quiz is meant to be a way to look inwards and reflect upon how we use social media. You can also take this quiz more than once, especially if you have a goal of going from the obsessive user to the more casual browser.

There is no right or wrong answer to any of the questions.

How often do you spend browsing through your social media accounts?	a. 1 - 2 hours
	b. 3 - 5 hours
	c. 6 - 8 hours
	d. 9 or more hours
You are out with your friends and you take a photo. You then...	a. Put your phone away to enjoy the activities.
	b. Text it to the friends you are with.

	c. Upload it for everyone to see.
	d. Take more photos to get the perfect shot.
Did social media impact your last or current relationship?	a. No.
	b. Kind of.
	c. Ask my friends, they will tell you.
Is going through your social media accounts part of your nightly bedtime routine?	a. No, I prefer to read or just relax.
	b. Only if I see a notification.
	c. Of course, how am I supposed to know what happened during the day?
	d. I scroll through my social media, and then I prepare what I'm going to post the following day.

When you get a notification, do you check it right away?	a. No, it will be there when I'm free.
	b. Depends on if it's a message or just random.
	c. Notifications? I am so quick that I don't get notifications.
You are on a trip where there is no reception, which means you won't be able to access social media. How do you feel?	a. Oh, I thought no one needed me, so I didn't get any messages.
	b. As long as someone knows where I am, that's good enough.
	c. My plan means I'm covered everywhere.
	d. #FirstWorldProblems I'll buy a reception booster.

Are you ready for your results?

If you answered **mostly A** - social media has little to no impact on your overall life and well-being. People who identify with a majority of A's see that social media has neither a hindrance nor benefit to their daily life. Whether you have reception in the middle of a forest or if you share that photo a month after the fact, most people who pick A typically have a good and healthy relationship with social media.

For those who answered **mostly B** - if you happen to open up your Facebook feed or not, it doesn't really matter to you. If someone likes your post or comments, it doesn't do much to your self-esteem or ego. People who select B have an understanding of social media in that they may have used it in excess in the past, and now they have decided to put restrictions on themselves. There is a lot of self-control, whether it be a conscious decision or not.

For **mostly C** respondents of the quiz - you are active enough on social media that you have mastered the perfect time to post for maximum engagement. You would rather not find yourself without connection. A lot of time is typically wasted by C responders on social media, even though those who answered C may say they have a good balance of when to put their phone down. People who answered C may be on the verge of addiction or dependency on social media.

For those who selected **mostly D**, social media is just as part of their daily routine as brushing their teeth or breathing. The thought of not having access to Facebook, Snapchat, or Tik Tok can seem stressful, and not being able to share or receive feedback is also stressful, if not anxiety-filled. Respondents of D find great emotional and mental support and benefits from their online presence, and any lack of exposure to their virtual world can lead to a state of depression.

It's important to remember that this quiz is not meant to shame or make you feel bad about your social media habits, but instead, this quiz is meant to showcase your current browsing style. Sometimes it takes seeing how much time we spend online to see how much we need to take a break for our own well-being. Not only is it important for that front, but disconnecting is a way of living in the moment.

Your Well-Being and Social Media

After completing the quiz, you should better understand how your life overall is being affected by your social media use.

It can be helpful to see how each area of your well-being is impacted by the excess use of social media.

Time Wasting

In your busy life, it is okay to 'waste' some of your time. Activities like watching TV, surfing the web, and going on social media can all be considered time-wasters. Spending a little bit of time each day doing activities like this is okay because everyone needs some downtime. These things are not necessarily time-wasters because they can be considered therapeutic activities. However, when the time spent begins to drag on from minutes to hours, it becomes a problem.

Wasting too much time on social media can have very negative impacts. If you are a student, you may notice that you have less and less time to study and complete assignments. Homeowners, you may notice that chores around the house don't get done because you got lost in your newsfeed. Parents, you may see that the time spent with your kids is balanced between your phone and their activities. Social media is designed to hook you in, and it can do an outstanding job in that department. Putting off other more important activities for your socials is usually a very negative thing.

Withdrawal

When you spend so much of your time on social media, you may notice that the world around you changes. Perhaps you used to hang out with friends regularly, visit coffee shops, or participate in sports activities. If you look back at the past few months, do you still do all these things?

There are a couple of reasons that social media can cause you to withdraw from others. The first is time. Let's say you have plans with friends. You take a shower and then start to get ready to go. But before you do, you sit down on your bed and pull out your phone. You think you will be on your phone for only five minutes, and then suddenly hours have passed. Now you are so comfortable, you don't feel like getting ready to go out, so you cancel on your friends. Scenarios similar to this may be happening somewhat regularly. In this case, social media is causing you to withdraw.

You may also be experiencing withdrawal from friends or family because of how social media is making you feel about yourself. How do you feel about yourself when you scroll through your newsfeed? Do other people's posts make you feel jealous? Or do other people's posts make you feel like you are not good enough? Or like you aren't attractive? All of these feelings are very real results of spending too much time and energy on social media. They can cause you to withdraw because you feel so poorly about yourself.

Another reason for withdrawal is secrecy. You may be using social media to engage in secret behavior or relationships. Your in-person life may begin to take a back seat to an online experience. It can be very easy to get consumed by your online persona because it's likely that you are doing this to fulfill hidden needs or desires. The pleasure you get from being online outweighs the joy you get from seeing your friends and family. Therefore, you end up withdrawing from your in-person life.

Changes in Behavior / Mood Swings

Extensive social media use can cause you to partake in activities that are outside of your norm. People post photos on socials that make their life look intriguing and exciting. It can motivate you to find activities that replicate that type of thrilling story. While stepping outside of your comfort zone can be a very positive thing, you may be engaging in questionable, unsafe behavior depending on the activity.

Social media is also filled with individuals expressing their trials and tribulations. Some of the people you follow may consistently post upsetting photos or statuses. Though they are talking about their own lives, it can still take an emotional toll on you, draining you of energy. It can cause you to feel sad, angry, or vengeful. Again, these feelings can be positive if it motivates you to strive for positive change. However, it can also lead you down a road of depression and despair.

When you are on social media all the time, you may notice your feelings going up and down in conjunction with the posts you read. When you read something happy, you feel good. When you read something sad, you feel frustrated. Other posts may make you feel jealous, angry, or left out. All of these emotions can then transfer into your real life, causing mood swings.

Mood swings are challenging for both you and your close company to deal with. Everyone experiences them from time to time, but when they become consistent, it is a problem. It is exhausting to find yourself happy one minute and drained the next. Additionally, while your family may try to support you through it, they are likely to become frustrated when their attempts don't work. No one likes to be part of a hostile environment, and you may be creating one based on the ups and downs of your moods.

Eating Disorders

When you spend time looking at others' pictures, you may begin to judge your own body. Instagram, Snapchat, and Twitter are flooded with people who take exquisite photos of their bodies—flaunting what are often unrealistic curves and muscles. These photos are usually taken at a clever angle and with ideal lighting. They often have a filter added as well. You may know these pictures are not accurate depictions of how that person looks, yet you find yourself envious anyway.

The jealousy you feel may cause you to take drastic measures. Your desire to have the body you see on your screen may become your sole focus. Perhaps you try to exercise and find that it doesn't work, at least not fast enough. So instead, you turn to dangerous eating behaviors.

To look just as skinny as the person on your screen, you may decide to skip some meals. After all, taking in fewer calories is a quick way to lose weight. You may also purposely vomit up what you do eat in order to conceal your behavior. Alternatively, you may eat a large portion of food in short amounts of time and then immediately purge to get it out of your system. Your methods may also be different from this. But, when you become obsessed with what you eat, consume only tiny portions, or purge what you do eat, you may be suffering from an eating disorder.

Often, eating disorders are only associated with people who skip meals in order to lose weight. However, compulsive overeating can also be brought on by social media addiction. Eating is a method many people use to soothe their upsetting thoughts. If your time on socials makes you feel bad about yourself, you may try to alleviate the mental discomfort with unhealthy food. The more you do this, the more unhealthy you become. Overeating often makes people feel a sense of guilt and shame, which may slowly cut you off from other people. Then, you turn to social media to connect with people because it's easier to connect online rather than in person. And so, the cycle starts all over again.

Lack of Sleep Due to Online Activity

Sleep is one of the most critical factors in your overall well being. Being properly rested allows you to focus at school or work. It improves your mood and increases your attention span. A good night's rest also helps to improve the appearance of your skin.

Sleep is necessary for your physical health, as well. The body needs time to rest and regenerate in order to reach peak performance levels.

Unfortunately, sleep is one of the first things affected by social media addiction. One of the most significant factors here is that many people use a phone, a tablet, or some sort of portable device. Many people lie in their beds on their device, meaning to go to sleep but getting lost in the world on their screen. You may think it's just a few minutes, but then several hours have passed, keeping you up later than you should be.

To make matters worse, being exposed to blue light right before sleeping is counterproductive to achieving rest. You may have the best of intentions, trying to go to bed early. You may even put down your phone after only a short amount of time. And yet, you still find you cannot sleep. This is because the blue light on your device stimulates the brain. So instead of drifting off into a peaceful dream state, you lie awake. Since you can't sleep, you pick up your phone and start browsing through your social media. Again, you stay up too late.

Lack of sleep is directly related to poor performance at work or in school. It can make you more moody, causing you to be easily irritated. The importance of a good night's rest cannot be overstated. And yet, your social media addiction can get in the way of that every single night, causing you to be in a perpetual state of overtiredness.

Desire for Attention

"Likes" may have been introduced as a way to show positive reinforcement. However, they have become a measure of self-esteem. Many people post photos or statuses with the goal of garnering as much attention and as many "likes" as possible. The anticipation of how many "likes" you get and the disappointment when you don't get them can be emotionally damaging.

When your photos are not getting the responses that you had hoped for, you have three options:

1. Accept it, understanding that "likes" should not change your self-esteem or personal happiness.
2. Feel bad about yourself, making you feel self-conscious and upset.
3. Post another, racier photo to get more "likes."

The first response is the most ideal, though challenging for many to achieve. The second can be very damaging to your self-esteem, and yet happens to people all the time. The third can lead to poor decision making and finding yourself in compromising positions. Unfortunately, it is an option many people turn to.

When you try to improve the response to your pictures, you may engage in behavior that is not good for you. For example, you may choose to post photos of how much alcohol you consume or wearing revealing clothing. You may find yourself hanging out with a crowd that you don't really like, burning your true friends in the process. When you make decisions about your life based on "likes" rather than fun, you can end up in a bad place both physically and mentally.

There is an alternative method of improving your "like" count, which is considered heinous, but happens every day. Some people find themselves posting about fictitious diseases or life problems. For example, someone may say they are suffering from a rare form of cancer or that their house was ruined in a hurricane. When online friends see posts like that, they often weigh-in to provide sympathy and support. Some even take it a step further and send money to help deal with the situation. Stories like this are harmful to everyone involved and only get worse as time goes on.

Lack of Other Interests

If you take a moment and look back at the past few months (or years) of your life, significant changes may have taken place in your life, specifically in your free time. Before using social media, did you have hobbies that you used to do? Perhaps you liked to go skiing, spend time in your garden, or knit. Have you noticed that you don't do these things as often? Or maybe you have turned down an option to partake in that hobby. Pre-social media, was that something you ever turned down?

Now, much of your spare time probably involves checking out how things are going online. You may spend long stretches of time scrolling through your newsfeed. When you are bored, you turn to your phone. When something exciting happens in your life, you turn to your phone. Before, you may have celebrated by buying a new tool for your hobby. Instead, now you just post about it on Facebook.

This is when your addiction starts to take control of your free time. You begin to lose interest in activities that you used to find enjoyable. You may also find that the way you seek pleasure is through your socials. Whether it's spending your time posting for "likes" or merely browsing, much of your free time is centered around social media.

You may also find that your mind wanders away to your online life, even if you aren't currently engaging in it. When you are out with friends or actually partaking in your hobby, you are mentally setting up your next picture post. Instead of enjoying the moment, you take 15 pictures to find the perfect image.

If this sounds like you at all, try this simple test. Look back through your pictures until you find a series of images that you took in an attempt to secure the best photo possible. Now that you see the pictures again, are they really that different? Did you really need to spend that much time obsessing over getting the right shot? It's likely that the first one or two photos were beautiful. Instead of enjoying your free time, you wasted it on a single picture.

Financial Stress

Your financial obligation to your social media may be a confusing one, especially since nearly all social accounts are free. However, if you suffer from an addiction or anxiety, you may be spending money on your online presence without realizing it.

Have you ever bought an outfit or a meal for the sole purpose of posting online? Or maybe you buy a new outfit because you already have a picture of every item in your closet. Alternatively, you may have spent more money than you should so you could set up a wicked shot. Or you want to make yourself look like you have more money than you do, so you buy an expensive watch that you really can't afford.

Putting your cash into items that you don't need can result from financial stress related to your social media addiction or anxiety. You want to appear to have this lavish life, so you spend money making that image appear to be true. This is a problem when you spend money you don't have. Money that you know should go to paying your water bill or reimbursing your sister, instead goes to buying a new pair of boots that you know will look great on Instagram.

In some extreme cases, you may have spent money to make up for a mistake you made. For example, perhaps you were checking your socials while driving. Unfortunately, this meant you were distracted and ended up hitting a car. Now, not only do you have to pay your deductible to have the repairs made, but your insurance may go up in the future. Depending on the accident, you may have earned demerit points from the police. An accident like this can follow your record for years, causing you to pay in both money and emotions for years to come. While this may seem excessive, scenarios like this are real and do happen.

There is one more type of financial cost that is connected to social media addiction. That is called an opportunity cost. A cost like this exists when you give up an opportunity to make money to spend time on socials. For example, have you ever turned down an extra shift at work because you are too comfortable lying in bed browsing your newsfeed? Or maybe you missed a call from your boss because you were wrapped up in what was happening on Twitter. Or, perhaps you passed up on work to take part in an activity you know would make your life look epic on Facebook. All of these scenarios result in you losing out on income because of your addiction. It is never a good idea to put social media ahead of your financial security.

Familial Problems

Your social media addiction may already have started to cause problems with your family. This makes sense because family members tend to be the first people who notice problems in your life. They can tell when something is wrong or when you have a change in behavior. They are also usually the ones to speak up first. Has a family member ever confronted you about your online habits? Have you ever ended up in an argument with them about it? Both of these are indicators that a problem exists.

Your family may have issues with your social media use in a few ways. Firstly, and very commonly, when you spend time with them, are you participating in the activity, or are you hiding behind your phone? Do you miss parts of the conversation because you are so wrapped up in what's on your screen? This is a big problem for many people who have a social media addiction. The brain cannot focus on two things at once, so you are sucked into your phone. This type of behavior is extremely bothersome for those with whom you are supposed to be spending time with.

Another reason your family may have problems is due to how you interact online. Are you a different person in your social media presence than you are in real life? Do you treat them differently online than you do in person? It is very common for people to be different behind a screen than in person. There is a degree of anonymity online that makes people act in a way they never would in person. This can be very frustrating for a family member to watch, especially if your online persona behaves differently when in direct contact with family. Has your family stopped engaging with you online? This is an indicator that your online life is a problem.

Finally, do you have a secret life online? Are there accounts that you would be embarrassed for anyone to find out about? Having a certain degree of privacy is okay; everyone needs to have that. However, are you engaging in activities that would cause problems in your relationship? If you hide something from your spouse and work hard to conceal it, your online activity is probably causing issues in your real life. Many people can sense when secrets are being kept from them, even if they don't tell you. Also, you are probably acting differently, even if you don't realize it.

Friendship Issues

Issues your social media addiction causes with your friendships may be very similar to any familial matters. However, friends are not family, so your relationship can be more complicated. It is much easier for a friend to cut you out of their lives. Have you noticed that your friend circles have changed? It could have something to do with your social media.

Friendships are delicate relationships that need cultivating. It is essential to treat your friends as you want to be treated. However, your social media activity may have resulted in an unfair dynamic. For example, posting pictures where you look great, but your friend doesn't, isn't a very nice thing to do. It may be tempting because you look so good, but that can be a very quick way to hurt your friendship. When you start putting your social media profile in front of your friendship, there is a problem.

Another friendship issue you may face is through the comments you make. Do you say nice things on your friends' profiles, or do you make fun of them in a mean way? Remember that social media is public; teasing them online is the same thing as teasing them to their face. It may seem like it is all in jest, especially if others are posting similar comments. But what you say online is just as hurtful, if not more, as it is in person. When you make comments on a friend's social media to improve your own online persona, your addiction is affecting your friendship.

Trust is a significant factor with your friends. When it is broken, it's hard to get back. Have you ever broken promises to your friends? Perhaps you posted something you promised you wouldn't. This is a breach of trust. Actions like this can cause a rift in a friendship that is so severe your relationship ends.

Problems at Work or School

Social media addiction can seep into your work. It can cause such severe problems that you get disciplined for your behavior, or even worse, fired. It may seem like an extreme reaction, but if your productivity begins to dwindle to a point where you are no longer an effective employee, you can lose your job.

When you are at work, do you find that you check your phone often? While you should be busy working, are you browsing your newsfeed? You may not think you spend very much time doing it, but it may be more than you realize. Your coworkers may crack jokes about it or even call you out in person. Has your boss ever told you that you need to spend less time on socials and more time working? This is a problem.

Social media is one of the first things potential employers check when you are interviewing for a new job. Have you ever gone to an interview, thought you did well, and then never received a callback? This could be because of your social media. Your content may be shocking to an employer. Or, maybe they notice what time you make posts. Is it often during the workday? How frequently do you post? These scenarios mean that you are missing out on potential jobs because employers think you are going to come into the workplace and spend the whole day on your phone.

If you are in school, your learning may be affected too. Have you ever been in trouble for having your phone out in class? That is a common occurrence, but how many times have you been told to put it away? When you just cannot seem to keep your phone in your pocket, it is beginning to affect your schoolwork.

Being so attached to browsing your social media means you miss the lessons your teacher is giving. Not having essential information means you won't do as well on a test or miss hearing an important deadline. From here, you may notice your grades slipping. All because you felt the urge to check your socials.

Some schools have such strict rules that you can be suspended for being warned too many times. All of this goes on your permanent record, meaning you may not get into the university or college of your choice. It can be hard to grasp, but every action has a consequence. When you are in school, your decisions matter. You may be selling yourself short of a bright future because you are wrapped up in socials.

Physical Health

Another faction of your life that can be impacted by social media is your physical health. This is not one that most people associate with their addiction, but it can be directly affected.

Social media is ripe with pictures showing people looking their very best. It used to be that only models, actors, and singers were airbrushed. Ads, commercials, and movies were filled with people who looked too good to be true. Nevertheless, many people felt compelled to look that way. It was unrealistic to look like someone who is paid thousands of dollars to look good, and pays even more to have their photos touched up, and yet, it happened every day. Now, with the invention of filters, people you know post photos looking like supermodels.

Social media gives people an unrealistic expectation of what they should look like. Even though you know it's not real, you still feel compelled to look perfect. This may cause you to partake in unhealthy diets, take untrustworthy diet pills, or buy experimental products. All of these are unsafe, and you probably know it. But your desire to get "likes" outweighs your physical health.

Your physical health may also be affected by your desire to take risks. Everyone has seen photos of people leaning over a mountain's edge or sticking their hands in a lion's mouth. This behavior is not safe and can cause terrible health issues. Yet, the urge to snap the photo outweighs the voice in your head. Keep in mind, you may even be violating laws and regional rules in place because your need feels more important.

You may also find yourself drinking alcohol, smoking, or doing drugs because you want to post a cool photo. If you are too young to be doing those, or if they are illegal, your physical health is being affected. Rules and laws are in place for a reason. This includes the legal drinking age and consumption amounts. Any time you put your health at risk to look cool, you are potentially making life-altering decisions.

Spiritual Health

Social media addiction can impact your spiritual health. Depending on your spiritual beliefs, this can mean either your religion or the set of values you follow. Either way, you may have noticed that your spirituality has fallen by the wayside recently.

If you look through your social media, can you find pictures of yourself engaging in behavior that violates your spiritual guidance? It may have started small, perhaps skipping a prayer session or forgoing a meditation, and then grown into something else. You may find yourself behaving in an overtly sexual way to get "likes" in a photo or excessively drinking. The behavior you used to avoid may become commonplace because of how much attention your photo received.

Do you feel at peace the way you used to? Do you feel a connection to your spiritual guidance, or has that been lost over time? Do you still talk to the same circle of people, or have you cut them out because you know they would disapprove of your behavior? What is your support system like? Do you have people you can turn to in times of need? Does your life still have a purpose, or do you not know why or what you are doing?

Negative answers to any of these questions can mean that your spiritual health has been affected by your social media.

Mental Health

Your mental health is one of the most critical aspects of your overall well-being. When your mind is overwhelmed and occupied, happiness and peace of mind are hard to come by. Instead, you may feel overwhelmed and stressed out. It can be hard to get out of bed and start the day. You may be able to function in your daily life, but just barely.

Social media addiction can take a serious toll on your mental health. Your mind gets occupied with checking your socials and making sure your profile is fascinating. This means that much of your mental energy is taken up by social media, leaving little room for anything else, including self-care.

Trying to keep with the latest trends or look picture-perfect all the time can result in personal neglect. Instead of caring for yourself in a comforting, compassionate way, you obsess over how you look and how others perceive you. You can lose your sense of self because you want to appear to be something you aren't.

Do you notice that your moods change quickly? Or do you feel depressed about your life? Do you compare yourself to others? Are you embarrassed about your experience, so try to cover it up with your posts? Have you ever felt so badly about your life that you have tried to hurt yourself? All of these can be the negative impacts of social media on your mental health.

Overall Impact

Your social media addiction may be present in your life in more ways than one. It is likely that you suffer from at least one, if not several, of the above impacts. Reading through, you can see how unhealthy social media can be in your life. It can take over to the point that it becomes unmanageable, affecting your everyday life and well-being.

That is not to say you need to cut socials out of your life entirely. Many people function well by understanding how to balance social media and a life outside of it. Even if you are very deep into your addiction, it is possible to heal and move forward.

To move forward from your addiction, you need to adopt a positive self-talk strategy. Self-talk is the voice in your head that reinforces your thoughts and actions. Self-talk is one of the biggest influencers in your brain. Even if you feel good about an accomplishment, negative self-talk can bring you down. It can remind you of all your flaws and the reasons you don't deserve happiness or acceptance. Self-talk is very powerful, so you need to learn how to control its narrative.

At this point in reading, you may be frustrated or even infuriated with yourself. Learning about how your life is being impacted can be very upsetting. That voice in your head may be telling you all about how it's your fault that social media took over your life. You may even be running a replay of all the bad things that have taken place in your life because of your addiction. You may be counting the friends you lost or the job you didn't get. Do not listen to that voice! Feeling bad about yourself will not move you forward out of your addiction.

In Chapter 8, you will learn more about overcoming your addiction and moving forward with your life. While you read, remember that you need to focus your mind on positive self-talk.

Chapter 8:

How to Recover From it All

"When everything seems like an uphill struggle, just think of the view from the top" - Anonymous

At this point, you are likely wondering, 'How do I make the necessary changes to recover from my social media addiction?' Up until now, your world has been defined by social media, constantly checking for updates, posting filtered photos, and striving for as many likes as possible. Remember not to beat yourself up for what you have been doing previously. Social media is designed to hold your attention, so you were only doing what you were intended to do.

Now is the moment to redefine how you spend your time. Yes, it is going to be difficult at first. But with effort and determination, you can find success. It will get more manageable along the way, and it won't be so difficult to overcome the temptations. Keep in mind that many small steps equal giant leaps. So just keep chipping away, and eventually, you will be able to live your life without social media.

Methods for Detoxing Your Brain and Recovery

There are several methods you can use to help you move forward. Some may work very well, while others may not be so effective for you. That's okay; everyone is different, so what works for one person may not for you. Read through the approaches to understand what each entails. Then, try the ones that appeal to you. It may take some trial and error, and it may be a combination of these methods. Remember, not all methods are going to appeal, but as long as you give it a shot, that is what matters.

Discover Your True Self

Through your social media addiction and anxiety, you may have lost your sense of self. Or maybe you have never truly found yourself. Don't feel bad about it. Many people search for years to discover who they are.

Overcoming and detoxing your addiction starts with learning about yourself. What are your needs? What do you like? What are you good at? Who are you? The journey of self-discovery is not a quick one, but it should be exciting. This action may take you a number of years to fulfill, but that is okay. It is better to do it right than to rush it.

While everyone takes a different path to find their inner self, here is a road map you can follow.

1. Spend quiet time with yourself. Stop using television, social media, or any other activity to distract yourself from silence. Being alone with yourself can be scary. However, it is necessary to get to know yourself. Be quiet and listen to your thoughts. At times, you may have negative self-talk, but as you get more comfortable, that is going to go away.

2. Understand who you are, not who you want to be. Most people have a clear idea of who they want to be. The problem is, you just aren't that person - but that is okay! You don't need to be anyone other than who you are.

That's not to say you can't work towards making improvements, but you don't need to change your personality or likes and dislikes. Try taking a personality quiz to unlock elements of yourself that you cannot describe or don't know how to define.

3. Uncover what you are good at and what you are not so good at. Everyone has strengths and weaknesses. Being able to define them helps you learn more about yourself and can serve you well in your career and everyday life.

This process can take some time and will likely include trial and error.

A career assessment test can be a good way to understand your strengths and weaknesses. It can also reinforce whether you are on your best career path or give you an idea of something that may be better suited to you. Even if you aren't looking for a career change, a good quiz can be an indicator of what you are good at. Read Chapter 10 Resources to find some suggestions on career and personality quizzes you can take.

4. Unlock your passions and desires. When you find and follow your passions, your life becomes more fulfilling. You will find that your mood improves and you feel happier when you are spending your time doing something you enjoy. Of course, the goal is to work at a job that satisfies your passion. However, this is not always possible. Sometimes your passion cannot make you enough money to survive, or it is simply not a practical career. If this is the case, take up your passion as a hobby. Make sure to dedicate a small amount of your paycheck to your love.

If you don't know what you are passionate about, try taking the quiz in Chapter 10.

5. Talk to your friends, family, or your employer. It is natural not to be aware of all aspects of your personality. Being self-aware is a learned skill. Try asking people you trust about what they perceive your strengths and weaknesses to be. Ask them to be honest. At first constructive criticism can be very hard to hear. Know that it is not a personal attack. If you can listen with an open mind, you can make improvements in your life to serve you better.

Finding Your Motivation

Everyone talks about motivation and how important it is. Motivation is the driving force behind everything you do. Have you noticed when you complete a task because you have to, you never put quite as much effort into it? But when you are doing something by choice, you put in all your effort, and the result is exceptional? That's motivation at work.

Your success with overcoming your social media addiction is tied to your motivation. If you don't really want to change your behaviors, you aren't going to.

So, how do you find your motivation?

Follow the steps listed below to define your cause and stick to your plan.

Set a goal. What do you want to get out of this process? Is it to spend less time on social media? Is it to spend more time with others in person? Is it to stop comparing yourself to others? Whatever it is, write it down. Your goal should be specific and measurable. For example, if you want to spend less time on socials, give yourself a number of minutes you are working towards.

Find your inspiration. Why do you want to do this? Will it improve your self-esteem? Or maybe it's to help you save money. Find a reason you can fall back on when your motivation begins to wane.

Write down your goal and your inspiration. Writing it down helps to solidify the idea. There is a mental connection your mind makes when you put pen to paper.

Post your goal and inspiration somewhere you can see it every day. The more you see the purpose in your own handwriting, the more motivated you will be to achieve that goal. Try posting it on a mirror, your fridge, or your computer. Anywhere that you see often is a good idea.

Share your goal with a friend or family member. They can help hold you accountable if you slip up. Plus, it's nice to be able to share your struggles with someone who can listen with a sympathetic ear.

Track your progress. Find a way to represent your goal visually. Seeing your progress is a great way to give yourself some extra encouragement. Try plotting your progress on a graph or giving yourself check marks every time you take a step forward. Go with whatever visual representation works best for you.

Reward yourself. Break up your goal into smaller checkpoints. When you reach one, reward yourself.

When you follow these steps, you can uncover what your motivation is. Sometimes following through with this exercise can help you uncover something about yourself that you may not have known or realized yet. In a way, this is what I hope readers will get from this book and the journey of disconnecting and detoxifying from social media. A journey to learning who you are, and what motivates and excites you. More importantly, I hope that on this journey readers find a way to reconnect to what matters the most to them.

Develop Coping Skills

Coping skills are defined as the behavioral, emotional, or mental tools that help you focus and find perspective when dealing with difficult situations. Your coping skills should be taken into consideration here for two reasons.

First off, are you using social media as a coping skill? Perhaps you are struggling with some issues that are difficult to face, so you log on to your socials to forget. It is so easy to sweep your thoughts under the rug by getting lost in something else.

Secondly, moving away from social media is going to be a difficult transition, during which you may feel loss, frustration, anger, or a host of other emotions. You are going to need coping skills to make it through this with success.

Here is how you can develop coping skills to deal with your social media addiction or anxiety.

1. Breathe. When you feel anxious, stop, and breathe. Breathe deeply in and out while counting to ten. When anxiety creeps up, your heart starts to race, and blood rushes to your head. Breathing will slow your heart and allow you to think more clearly at the moment.

2. Get some perspective. Many people jump to worst-case scenario modes in their brains. Don't beat yourself up for doing that, but train yourself to have healthier thoughts like, 'What other scenarios are more likely to happen?'

3. Problem solve. The feeling of no way out is overwhelming and suffocating. When you feel like there is no solution to your problem, your emotions can run rampant. Instead of letting this get to you, break down your massive problem into small manageable issues. Taking action and making small strides will make you feel

better. Then build on those small steps to solve the larger problem at hand.

4. Create positive habits. Positive habits, such as getting active or reading, are excellent ways to deal with a build-up of emotions. Not only can they help soothe your feelings, but they are good for your body and mind as well. Read the section on *Replacing Bad Habits with Good Ones* for tips for adopting better habits.

These skills may not be applicable to everybody. Some may find them helpful, while others may not. The point of this is to try to engage in a way that, when you find yourself in an uncomfortable situation, you have the tools to cope. Not only do you have the skills to cope, but you can move past the experience as well.

Resiliency is something that is learned through detoxifying our brain. For some, they may not realize how resilient they are until they overcome a challenge such as this; and this is a challenge worth celebrating! This notion of resiliency is, in essence, what helps those who have stepped away from social media to remain away, or rather create the boundaries and limitations of their online presence.

Daily Routines

Establishing a daily routine has a number of health benefits. On the surface, the thought of creating a routine may seem rigid and overly planned. However, understand that a routine is not a schedule but a pattern. Keep in mind that scheduling can have merits, especially for overcoming an addiction or bad habit. Read the section on *Time Management Skills* for more information about setting a schedule.

Routines are a way to create healthy habits and improve your overall wellbeing. A good routine makes sure you take care of all your mental, emotional, and hygiene needs. A pattern will also lower your stress level, which is something most people can benefit from.

Decide what your routine should include. For most people, this means going to bed and waking up at the same time each day - even on weekends. Getting the proper amount of sleep is essential and works wonders to restore your energy.

Your routine can also include eating a healthy breakfast, engaging in physical exercise or mental stimulation, such as reading a book or the newspaper. The point is to have an element in your routine that helps fuel your body and mind.

Another excellent item to include is 10 minutes of cleaning at the end of each night. Making sure your house looks tidy before you go to bed helps you wake up feeling refreshed. The same is true about making your bed in the morning. Making your bed starts your day off right, making you more productive throughout the rest of your day.

There is one more benefit of routines that you should keep in mind. Suppose you have children; following a routine sets a good example. Kids thrive on routine and learn by example. Kids pick up habits from their parents, so setting them up for success at a young age is important.

Think of the kids you see these days with an iPhone or an iPad and how much they would rather spend time playing games or chatting than going outside. As parents and adults, if we can set them on a foundation that allows them to make better decisions, we are putting them on a path of preventative measures. What measures? We are helping them realize that there is more to life than their screen. By helping them make wise decisions and setting a proper example of disconnecting, we show them how meaningful relationships come from being present, not absent.

Replacing Bad Habits with Good Ones

Your social media addiction and anxiety are likely laced with bad habits. These habits may seem insignificant but actually have a big impact on your daily life and self-esteem. Breaking these habits and replacing them with new healthy ones will improve your mental health and overall well-being.

You may think that your social media routines are not problematic, nor are they habitual. However, consider the following:

- When you first wake up in the morning, do you check your phone?
- Are you on social media right before going to bed at night?
- Do you find yourself checking your social media during work hours?
- When hanging out with family and friends, do you miss some parts of the conversation because you are on your phone?
- Have you ever checked your phone while driving?

To many people, these are seemingly normal behaviors - everyone pulls out their phone at work. But these actions can be quite damaging when you consider all of their negative consequences. For example, did you know that you probably aren't sleeping very well because of your habits? Or that your friends may be very bothered when you are on the phone while they are trying to talk to you? Identifying these poor behaviors and replacing them with better ones is an excellent strategy for overcoming your addiction.

The first step is to identify the behavior. Do you have triggers that initiate those actions? Are they part of your daily routine? Once you know what they are, you can work with them.

Next, come up with an alternative behavior you will launch into when you are tempted to check your social media. Maybe it's going for a walk or cooking a meal. It should be anything you can do to distract yourself from the temptation.

Enlist the help of a friend or family member to help get you through. Sharing your goals with someone else helps hold you accountable to someone other than yourself. This can be a good form of motivation to help stay on track.

Finally, try leaving yourself notes or reminders around your house. Put a sticky note on your mirror, in your bag, even on the back of your phone. It could say something like 'I'm not missing out on anything,' or 'I am happy with my life; I don't need validation from others.' Seeing these notes are great ways to stay on track.

Delete or Deactivate Your Accounts

Though it may seem drastic, deleting your accounts may be the best course of action. Sometimes cutting off the source of discomfort and temptation is the only way to move yourself forward.

Living through social media can give you a skewed view of reality. You can get this skewed sense of reality by browsing through the 'lives' of people you barely know or care about. Does it really matter to you what someone from high school is doing? When was the last time you spoke to them? Were you ever really their friend?

Alternatively, you may get anxious, trying to find the perfect picture to post. You may take the same photo again and again or add a filter until you look flawless. Social media can drive you to attempt to keep up with someone else's life. These behaviors are not healthy, nor do they allow you to live up to your true happiness. When you are always trying to look or seem more interesting, you cannot be truly happy.

The unfortunate thing is, you would probably be quite content with what you are already doing if you didn't have the stress of social media. You could enjoy lunch out with friends better if you didn't feel the urge to make it look so picture perfect. You wouldn't feel a constant need to make your life look so impressive.

Deleting or at least deactivating your accounts can bring you a sense of freedom. You can learn to enjoy the moment for what it is, rather than what it could look like to someone else.

This can be difficult for someone who is heavily influenced or rather impacted by social media; however, sometimes going the old-fashioned "cold turkey" approach is the best way to step back from social media. And, for those who find this thought too difficult to accept or do, remember that you can always get your account back. Yet, if you are truly serious about quitting and regaining some control back, why not challenge yourself?

Turn Off Notifications

Seeing that icon pop up on your phone can be a tempting moment. Who posted what? Is there a juicy piece of gossip? Has someone invited you to a party? The point of a notification is to draw you on to the social media site, not to let you know that someone is thinking about you.

More often than not, a notification is the site telling you that a friend posted something that may be of interest to you. It does not directly affect you, but the site wants to hook you in. You see the notification, and you click on it. Did it really have anything to do with you? Probably not. But now that you are here, you decide to scroll through your newsfeed. Suddenly, fifteen minutes have passed, and you haven't looked up from your phone. The notification accomplished precisely what it had intended. It brought you on to the platform when you otherwise had no intention of logging on.

To avoid getting sucked in, try turning off your notifications. It is easier to spend less time on social media when your phone is not always trying to draw you in. Remind yourself that, most of the time, notifications do not lead you anywhere productive.

If you are concerned about missing personal communications from friends, family, or work, only leave direct message notifications on. This way, you remain available, but don't get lost in useless alerts.

Do you want to challenge yourself? Put your device on sleep mode every night and see if you can go a night without thinking about or checking your notifications. Every night, why not extend the length of time your phone is on sleep mode and see how long you can last? This approach is suitable if you want to take a more cautious and slow approach. More importantly, it is also a way of helping you realize that your phone, those notifications, aren't as important or vital to your well-being as you think.

Re-evaluate Your "Friends" List

The total number of people on your friends list may seem to be an accomplishment. The higher the number, the more friends you have. But if you really take a hard look at your 'friends', you will probably discover that that is simply not true. Many of these people are probably only acquaintances, or they may be people you knew in a former life. For example, they could be people you went to high school with, but never even spoke to. Or they may be someone you worked with years ago but never kept in touch with. Though having a high friend count may seem important, it may be more harmful than good.

Watching the life of other people may create a feeling of resentment, jealousy, or envy. You want what they have. But keep in mind that people only post what they want you to see. Do you often see photos of the same person going on vacations or eating out at elegant restaurants? This seems like a wonderful life, but take a moment and analyze it. What do these expensive habits cost? Can they really afford that lifestyle, or are they racking up debt? What you see in photos may not show the whole story, so try not to get hung up on what someone else has.

The most effective way to overcome feelings of social media envy is by pairing down your friends list. Start by eliminating people you barely know. Then move on to people who you do not keep in contact with and have no intention of ever speaking to. You may be amazed by how many people this eliminates.

If you are willing to take it a step further, start analyzing the friends, family, and coworkers you are left with. Do any of them post statuses or opinions that you find objectionable? Or maybe the way someone comments on your posts always makes you feel bad about yourself. Take a moment and really think about who you have on your list. Keep only the people who bring you up in life, not those who bring you down.

If you feel like you cannot delete someone because of social obligations, try to block their posts and notifications. This way, you still appear as friends, but you do not have to be in tune with what they post.

Deleting friends may be one of the hardest things you do. But filling your news feed with only posts that make you feel positive can have a liberating effect on your anxiety. Watch how your self-esteem improves when you are no longer bombarded by negativity.

Tackling Loneliness and Boredom

Many people turn to the internet and social media because they are lonely or bored. Perhaps you live in a place where you feel left out - like no one around you has common interests, or you have trouble making friends. Social media can be a wonderful escape for anyone living in these scenarios.

Boredom is another reason for browsing through social media. When you have nothing to do, picking up your phone and getting lost in the online world seems like a good way to while away the hours. Social media can be useful for boredom or loneliness, but it can also cause addiction and anxiety problems. Seeing other people hanging out with friends, visiting theme parks, or traveling around the world can make you feel even worse about your own situation. The stimulation and connection you went looking for ended up doing you more harm than good.

When you feel bored or lonely, try tackling the problem with a different method.

First, learn to enjoy your own company. There are many solo activities that can be fun; you just need to be in the right frame of mind. For example, if you are interested in cooking, find a recipe you have always wanted to try and make it: research specialty or local stores in your area where you can buy the ingredients. Or, if you are more technically inclined, try visiting an internet cafe to play your favorite game.

Both of these can be individual activities. However, when you do them a little differently than usual, you can expand your horizons and possibly network with other people. You never know who you are going to meet at the grocery store or the internet cafe. Even if you don't meet someone, you are getting out of the house and doing something you enjoy. This tackles both your boredom and your loneliness.

Learn to enjoy these times on your own. It builds your confidence and serves you better than going on social media.

Time Management Strategies

Another strategy you can try is managing the amount of time you spend on social media. Reducing how long you spend browsing or setting out specific windows of time to go on can help you take back control of your life.

If you are a person who thrives on structure, create a schedule for yourself that outlines how long and when you can be on social media. If a schedule is not your thing, but you need some boundaries, come up with a time limit for your browsing.

Your schedule can look something like the following:

7:00 am: Wake

7:15 am: Breakfast and get ready for work

8:00 am: Commute

8:30 am: Begin workday

10:30 am: Coffee break, browse social media

10:45 am: Back to work

12:30 pm: Lunch and check social media

1:00 pm: Back to work

3:00 pm: Break

3:15 pm: Back to work

4:30 pm: End of workday, commute home

6:00 pm: Make and eat dinner

7:30 pm: Relax and browse social media

8:30 pm: Put phone away

10:00 pm: Bedtime

Notice that with the schedule, you do not check your socials until your day is well underway. Additionally, you are not checking them at every break possible. The goal is to disassociate your downtimes with being online. Also, take note that you are giving yourself a long stretch to check things out in the evening. However, the time comes after you have finished your responsibilities for the night and well before you go to sleep.

As a bonus to reducing your social time, you will probably end up sleeping better. Being on your phone or in front of blue light right before bed can lead to poor sleep cycles. Do something calming like reading a book or taking a bath before bed instead of checking your phone. You may be surprised by how much easier it is to sleep when your brain is calm.

For those who feel this schedule is too rigid, try a different time management skill. Give yourself a time limit on how long you can spend on social media at a given time. Perhaps it's 15 minutes; maybe it's 30. You need to be the judge of that. Also, give yourself a limit for the number of times you can go on. Keep in mind that the longer you give yourself in a single stretch, the fewer times you should be checking.

For example:

Let's say you give yourself 15 minutes per browsing cycle. Then you should limit your number of checks to 6 per day. In total, you would be spending 1.5 hours per day on social media.

Let's say you instead choose 30 minutes per check. Then you would limit yourself to 3 checks per day. Again, your total time spent is 1.5 hours.

Creating a schedule or time limits may be difficult at first, primarily if you are used to spending a significant number of hours online. If needed, start with a more generous amount of time and wean down as you get more used to the restrictions.

Rediscover the 5 Senses — Live in Living Color

When you spend so much of your time in the online world, you are forgetting the joy of using all of your senses. Looking at a picture of beautifully plated food is not the same as tasting it. Seeing a photo of trees in the fall is not the same as walking through a trail to see moss-covered boulders and smell the crisp autumn air while fallen leaves crunch under your feet. Living your life in front of a screen robs you of the wonder of in-person experiences.

Closing your computer or putting down your phone gives you back the ability to enjoy your physical world. Instead of seeing what other people are doing, go out and do it yourself. When you go to a restaurant, look at your dish and appreciate how carefully the vegetables are plated alongside your seared steak. Take a minute to smell the delicate spices used to enhance the flavor. Notice how the knife cuts through the meat like butter. Savor every mouthful of your meal. But don't take a picture. Don't post anything on social media. Don't tag your location. Just enjoy the moment for what it is.

This is an example of living with your five senses. It's about being present in the moment. Often, this is called mindfulness. If living mindfully is new for you, there are a few ways you can practice. It is surprisingly difficult to live in the moment, so it does take a bit of work. Once you get it, you will see your stress start to melt away while you begin to enjoy life more.

Here are a few tips for living mindfully:

1. Exercise regularly. Only focus on the task at hand while you exercise.

2. Practice mindful breathing. Mindful breathing can decrease negative self-talk and reduce anxiety.

3. Spend time outside. This can be as simple as going for a walk around your block.

4. Learn and practice active listening. When having a conversation with someone, use all of your focus and energy to pay attention to what they are saying.

5. Wake up earlier than you need. Avoid rushing in the mornings. Wake up 15 minutes earlier than you need so

you have time to get ready slowly or spend a few minutes enjoying a bit of peace and quiet.

Rewiring the Brain

Overcoming your social media addiction or anxiety may require some brain rewiring. This is not nearly as drastic as it sounds. It's more about finding new ways to look at situations. When done right, you can learn to deal better with disappointment, gain confidence, and overcome your fears. It can open you up to new experiences and enhance your life, not to mention mend relationships that were impacted or affected by your addiction to social media.

Now that you are going to be spending time away from your phone, you need a new way to occupy your time. You also need a form of distraction because the temptation to look at your socials is going to be there for a while. Rewiring your brain for these situations is possible; it just takes some work.

Here are some strategies you can employ to rewire your thinking.

- Take up an instrument. Learning to play music has been proven to boost your concentration and improve your coordination. It also improves your mood. Music can also help enhance cognitive function later in life. So learning music now can help as you age.

- Learn a new language. Speaking another language helps your brain think in a new way. It can help improve your memory, motor skills, increase your vocabulary, improve your reading comprehension, and improve your problem-solving skills. It also creates an opportunity to meet new people and open up new job prospects.

- Get some exercise. Exercise is good for the brain and the body. Overall, your body functions better. It also makes people feel more confident in themselves. Additionally, you will notice that you sleep better at night and are in a better mood throughout the day. If you need extra motivation to work out (many people do), consider joining a walking group or going to the gym with a friend. Exercise then creates an opportunity for socializing in person and forging new relationships.

- Play a video game. While this may seem like odd advice, video games can be part of a mentally healthy lifestyle. Cooperative games teach teamwork and communication skills. They also improve your problem-solving abilities. Interestingly, video games can give you a healthy perspective on dealing with loss. They create resiliency and encourage you to try again after a failure instead of giving up.

These tips for rewiring your brain may seem like they don't align directly with social media addiction and anxiety. However, realize that your mind is a complex place. Factors that seem separate are, in fact, connected. Merely telling yourself that you must stop your social media habits is not going to work. You need to replace that time with something enjoyable and productive. Get the most out of your life by taking up activities that enhance your experiences, body, and mind.

Priorities

Understanding and defining your priorities is essential for finding peace in your mind and your life. Your priorities determine how you spend your time, where you spend your money, and what you dedicate your energy to. Currently, your priorities may be somewhat misaligned if you spend so much of your time and energy on your social media accounts.

Having skewed priorities can cause several problems in your life. For example, you may struggle with goal setting because you don't know what you truly want. Even worse, you will likely struggle to follow through on your goals.

You may also have trouble planning ahead. Instead, you live in a repeatedly reactive mindset where you are always putting out fires rather than mitigating them. Being reactive means you may miss out on opportunities because you are too busy cleaning up a mess. When you finally solve one problem, the next already arises, and the cycle repeats. Living like this is exhausting.

One of the biggest problems with having undefined priorities is how you feel about yourself based on other people's opinions, what you see, or what you read. When you see what other people are doing on social media, it can make you want to have what they have. You may abandon your current path so you can recreate theirs. This is also true of the comments, or lack thereof, posted on your own wall. If you don't like what you read, you may devise new events to post about, not because you want to do them, but you want people to 'like' you doing them.

So, how do you define your priorities?

Write down a list of all the things you want to prioritize in your life. Ask yourself questions like:

- What are the things in my life I could not live without?

- What can I do, but want to do better?

- What about my life causes me pain? Why?

- What don't I have but truly desire?

Walk away from this list for a few days. Look at this again with fresh eyes. Does your list still seem accurate? If anything has changed, remove that item from your list.

Once you have taken a break from your list, narrow your list down to what you consider to be your top three to five priorities.

Put this list in somewhere you will see. Going forward, your decisions should be focused on these priorities. Do not engage in behavior that violates your focus, and remember why you made this list to start with. Sometimes being reminded of why we are doing something can help us to put our end-goal in perspective.

Finding Balance

To deal with your addiction and anxiety, you may need to find a balance between social media and the rest of your life. If you aren't cutting it out completely, you need to find a way to have it in your life without letting it overtake your time and emotions.

When you put your mind to it, finding balance can be simple. One of the first things you should do is carve out time to spend with your family and friends. Being with the people you care about in real life is much more rewarding than following their lives online. While you are with them, avoid being on your phone. Give the visit your undivided attention.

Next, learn to spend time alone. That advice appears several times throughout this book because it is crucial to your well-being. You are a valuable person with dynamic thoughts and an interesting perspective. Learn to love yourself and enjoy being with yourself. Healthy alone time is a good way to recharge your batteries. It gives you the time and ability to be the best version of yourself.

Another great way to find balance is by learning something new. Take a class, teach yourself a skill, or do something you have always wanted to try. This can lead to a new hobby, new friendships, or even a new passion. The bottom line is you need to find something that interests you, so you can spend your time doing it, rather than being on social media.

Setting Yourself Up for Success

Before you try any of these healing approaches, set yourself up for success. Attempting to make changes in your life without being realistic about the path forward can lead you to failure. You are about to make a significant change, so understand what that truly entails.

Understand you may have some failures. Like any other addiction, a dependency on social media is not easily overcome. There may be times that you slip up and check your newsfeed, no matter how hard you try to avoid it. You will experience cravings that are difficult to suppress.

Just imagine you meet up with a group of friends, and everyone is talking about what 'Johnny' posted last night. Or while riding the bus, you catch a glimpse of a funny meme circulating on Facebook. Each of these is a trigger that may cause you to relapse, and that is okay. We are human, and our emotions are sometimes beyond our control. Remember, rewiring our brain, relearning habits, takes time and patience. Be easy on yourself, and be kind as well.

Understand that relapsing is a natural part of fighting any addiction. Instead of denying you've relapsed or beating yourself up, accept that it happened. Acknowledge that you made a bad judgment call and get back on track where you left off.

It may also be helpful to have a plan for relapses going into your social media free world. What are you going to do if you log on when you aren't supposed to? Do you have someone in your support system that you can call to talk about it? Or perhaps you would prefer to write it in a journal. Any method that you choose is fair, so long as it works for you. Planning out your strategy ahead of time can get you back on track faster. It can also help you to avoid negative self-talk, which often causes more harm than good.

Celebrate your successes. Every time you do well or resist temptation, give yourself a pat on the back. Recognize all of the effort and hard work you are putting in, and don't downplay any of it. Celebrating your success feels good. Understand that you do not need anyone else to acknowledge what you have done. You can be your own advocate. That kind of thought process is good for your overall well-being and improves your self-esteem in other areas of your life.

Additionally, you can use your successes as motivation to continue. They show you that you can do it again because you have already done it in the past. This motivation is a great way to work through any anxiety you may feel when walking away from social media. And as a bonus, the lessons you learn about overcoming anxiety or fear can be used again in other areas of your life.

Have an answer ready. There are going to be people who have something to say about your choices. They won't understand your decision; they may criticize you or say something rather stupid. They may think you are overreacting or that social media cannot possibly cause a problem in your life. Do not let this derail you or second guess why you are making these changes. Accept that this is going to happen and prepare your answers ahead of time. You do not have to explain yourself or justify why you have made this choice to disconnect and detoxify. The decision to put your well-being first - mentally, emotionally and physically - is your decision, and yours only. Those who feel they have a say, should not be part of your journey, especially if they cannot respect your decision.

Your answer does not need to go into detail; it can be vague but to the point. For example, 'I'm deleting my accounts to improve my well-being. I look forward to connecting with you more in person or over the phone.' The goal is to give them an answer that satisfies their curiosity but shuts down any further discussion.

Be Patient with Yourself

Do not expect miracles. You are undergoing behavior modification, and this is going to take significant effort. You are essentially learning a new way to spend time with yourself. It is unrealistic to think that one day you are going to wake up, delete all of your accounts, and walk away from social media without ever thinking about it or having an urge to check your feed again. While few people may be able to quit cold turkey, they are still likely to experience cravings.

Embrace Positive Self-Talk

What does this mean? It means taking those "I can't do it" and "I'm not good enough" statements and turning them into "I can do this" and "I am good enough." You would be amazed at how changing the dialogue in our mind can make a difference. And, when it comes to social media, this is important. It is important because much of the pressures and expectations we see online push us to question whether or not we are good enough, whether or not we meet the perfect mold. The truth of the matter is, YOU are good enough. You don't need a "like," a comment, or a "share" to tell you otherwise.

Adopting a mentality of self-talk can be easier said than done, especially if you don't know how. Changing self-talk is about listening to your mind and analyzing whether it is a negative message. From here, you need to change the tone so it is positive or at least constructive.

For example, try to avoid thinking the following statements when you are browsing through social media:

1. Everyone else has a better life than me.
2. Nobody likes me because they don't "like" my posts.
3. Nobody will ever love me the way I am.
4. I have to look perfect in all my photos, especially since I don't look perfect in real life.
5. My body always looks terrible in pictures; I need a filter to look better.
6. My opinion does not count, so I should agree with everyone else.
7. I am not good enough the way I am; social media proves that.
8. I don't have as many people on my friends list as other people.
9. I am not worth it.
10. I can't and will never be any different.

Instead, replace these negative thoughts with positive ones like this:

1. My life is great the way it is. I'm glad others have a good life, too.
2. I don't need "likes" to make me happy with my life. I'm pleased with the "likes" I do get from my close friends and family.
3. I am a great person the way I am. I will find someone; I just have not met them yet.
4. I like my pictures to reflect on how I look in person. Nobody is perfect.
5. I respect my body the way it is. I don't need any filters because they don't represent the true me.
6. I am a dynamic person with interesting thoughts. I can share my opinion if I so choose.

7. I am good enough just the way I am.
8. I know everyone on my friends list personally. The only people on there are the people who I care about and who care about me.
9. I am worth it.
10. If I want to make changes in my life, I can. But I will only do so if I want to, and it makes my life better.

Changing your self-talk from negative to positive is possible, but it can be difficult. It takes effort and dedication at the beginning. When you hear yourself saying mean things, stop for a moment. Do not let the thought continue to brew. Then, think about how you can alter the words to make them more positive. Tell yourself the new, positive side of the conversation. Then, move forward with the better version in your mind.

So, *be kind to yourself.* Forgive yourself for having those thoughts about logging back onto your account. Don't beat yourself up when you pick up your phone with the hope of checking your social media. Avoid negative self-talk and, instead, be patient with yourself. The world is often not kind to people; don't continue that trend by being unkind to yourself as well. We may be our worst critic, but we can be our greatest advocate, and sometimes, when we are risking our well-being - mentally, physically, or emotionally - we need to take action and reassess why.

I have said it time and time again in this book, and the reason I do is because it is true. We can't let social media or our smart devices control us. We can't allow someone else's opinion of us to dictate how we are going to live. Break free, and find yourself again, but this time without social media and the selfies!

Chapter 9:

Conclusion

"Our greatest glory is not in never failing, but in rising up every time we fail"
- Ralph Waldo Emerson

Have you taken a breath of fresh air lately?

Have you stopped to smell the roses?

Have you taken the time to enjoy being in the moment rather than being preoccupied with your smart device?

If you have answered "yes" to the previous, congratulations, you have successfully taken the time to disconnect from social media. You have allowed yourself to be in the moment despite being bombarded and pressured by the various platforms. This may not have been a comfortable journey; it may not have been one you expected to undertake. However, when you stop and pause, do you notice a difference? Do you notice a change in your relationship with friends, family, and colleagues? Do you see the world with a different pair of lenses?

I began this book and journey looking at how I could provide an ounce of insight, guidance, and perspective when it comes to coping with social media and the many, sometimes hidden pressures and expectations. There has been a movement by the media and health professionals to push for regulation and to encourage users to create time restrictions on their exposure and usage. I hope that in these last few chapters, you have found some tips and helpful practices to ease the anxiety and roller coaster emotions that come with being transparent on social media.

Step by Step

From the quizzes and resources, it is essential to remember that results are not instant. One cannot expect that their fears, insecurities, or anxiety will be resolved overnight. It is a step-by-step process that has a roller coaster of high's and low's. For those who suffer from low self-esteem, or for those who have a mental disorder, the digital world of social media can be cruel and vicious. We become so blind to the obvious harmful and negative impact of social media on our personal and professional lives that we do nothing. We do nothing because we think it's normal to feel anxious and that it's normal to have toxic and harmful interactions online because they are online.

What we forget, and I hope I have brought to light through this book, is that there are people in our lives who become affected by our actions, or lack thereof. When we choose to go on our phones or smart tablets rather than engage in meaningful and real relationships face-to-face, we are hurting those who care about us.

Social media has the power to break up marriages, ruin relationships, and turn friends into enemies – that is, if we let it. In this book, I share with you the established research and facts that health and social professionals have discovered regarding the impact of social media on the mental, physical, and emotional well-being of its users.

When it comes to creating an awareness of our browsing or social media habits, no one wants to admit they have a problem. No one wants to feel like these platforms that were used to connect us with others, to keep us in touch with friends and family, are actually doing more harm than good. However, the truth is, sometimes, too much of a good thing is bad.

Do you remember when your parents would tell you to not to indulge too much in sugar? This principle is very much applicable to our social media habits. Too much time spent glorifying our lifestyle, glorifying our desires and wants, only leads to inner turmoil. Recognizing this may literally be painful. But, it is possible to put down your phone and not feel like you are missing out. My goal throughout this book is to help you see that the only thing you are missing out on is what is happening right in front of you.

Being plagued with anxiety, coming off an addiction, or living with the scars of one is never easy. It is a journey, to be sure. This book is meant to be your guide on that journey, with suggestions and insight from a step-by-step process for a life without dependence on "likes," or clout, or the need to be perfect - a journey of betterment.

Will there be obstacles down the road?

Of course!

Nothing in life is easy, especially when it is meant to help us be a better version of ourselves. So let's begin, continue, and remain on the journey to enjoying life and all it has to offer - offline, in living color. Soon enough you will discover that all the time you spent online wasn't as important or as essential as you thought. This perspective and life lessons are ones that we have to experience to truly understand.

The real world, where you can be your true self, is all around you. It is ripe with the potential for real, meaningful, and satisfying relationships.

Chapter 10:

Resources

If you, or someone you know, is experiencing a social media addiction or who is impacted by anxiety due to social media, here are resources that can be of assistance.

Remember, there is no shame in asking for help. More importantly, there is nothing wrong with admitting the impact that social media has on our lives.

When Facebook, Twitter, and Instagram came out, no one knew the impact social media would have on its subscribers. Hence, the push to provide users with support and relevant information.

Resources for Information or For Help

When it comes to these resources, remember it won't always be easy, but it won't always be like this. These resources are meant to be a place where you can find the necessary information and support you require. If you have never sought support or assistance in the past, here are some helpful tips to consider.

Seeking Resources for Information

If you or someone you know has a social media addiction or is suffering from anxiety or depression, consider looking for resources on the topic. Learn more about what they may be going through, and consider sharing the information with them.

When looking for such resources, consider the following:

Where is it From?

Thanks to the world wide web, anyone can publish anything, which can be dangerous when you are looking for information on mental health, addiction, and anxiety. When looking up information, be weary of publications that do not direct you to trusted and well-reputed sources. Typically, this means going to well-known organizations or medical treatment centers. For example, WebMD is known as a trusted site for information, as well as the Mayo Clinic. These are just two websites that share verified and truthful information.

Not only do they provide resources, but they can also offer support based on the need.

How Old is the Information?

Things are constantly changing. New research is always being shared with other medical professionals, as well as the public. When you are looking for information regarding your search, consider the age of the information because once things are on the internet, very rarely do they disappear or are they updated.

Something to note however, is if you are going to a reputable site, chances are the information is kept up to date. Nonetheless, it is still important to know when the information you are reading, or sharing was created. If we look at it from a social media addiction perspective, this is something that has only become a thing in the last decade; therefore, the information you find may either be new or limited. The internet is vast, and the side effects it has on people is even much more unknown and grander.

Check the date and check who is publishing the information.

Primary vs. Secondary Sources

Similar to the previous point of where it is coming from, the internet is known to "copy and paste" as a form of sharing information which is why considering the type of source that you are looking at is important. Will this require a bit more effort on one's part? Yes, but it is to ensure that the information you are reading, and sharing is in fact true and not false information.

For example, if you are reading an article on how to support someone with anxiety, you don't want to take the tips and start applying them, just to realize that the tips you are following are, in fact, not medically sound. Checking to see where the information you are following, or reading is coming from is important. Don't put yourself or the person you are helping at risk by taking ill-advice online.

Remember, the world wide web is vast, but that doesn't mean everything you read is kosher.

Seeking Resources for Help

If you are seeking resources to help someone or yourself, consider the following:

Anonymity

When seeking resources to provide support for an addiction, especially one like social media, it is important that the services or resources you seek provide the necessary privacy and anonymity. When patients seek help, the last thing they want is to be shamed or feel like they are being judged.

Most practices and treatment centers provide the necessary privacy that patients need.

It is also important that when searching for facilities or beginning the search that you consider who is involved in the treatment plan. For example, some facilities require friends and family members to be part of the healing process, while other facilities focus solely on the individual.

Costs

Depending on where one is seeking treatment, the costs are to be considered. Some facilities are funded by the government, while others are private therefore the patient and their family must pay out of pocket.

There are also some grants that may be available. For more information you can always reach out to the treatment center to see if they have any grants or funding options.

In the situation that you or the person you are helping is unable to afford such treatments, there are helplines that you can contact and they can help with the process of getting the necessary resources and support you need.

In-House or Out-Patient

When searching for treatment centers and options, there are two types that can be considered, in-house and out-patient.

In-house treatments usually result in the patient or the one seeking treatment to stay at the facility. In the case of a social media addiction, this allows the patient to disconnect fully. In a way this could be seen as quitting cold turkey; however, this is just one way of tackling such an addiction.

With in-house treatments, the patient works with doctors, counselors, and they are usually surrounded with other individuals who are also experiencing a similar addiction or trauma.

Outpatient treatments mean that the individual can be in the comforts of their home and support network, but for treatments they go to a facility or center.

This has its pros and cons. It is a pro because it costs less for the patient and their family, and it allows them to seek treatment while having the emotional and physical support of friends and family.

The downside to this however is that it may require more time and patience, especially if they struggle with disconnecting. The temptations may be much more available to an out-patient than that of an in-house patient. Another thing to note with an out-patient is that the support of medical staff and trained professionals is only available when they are at the center, otherwise, they only have the support of their family.

If neither in-house or out-patient is an option you or your family want, speak with a specialist to see if there are alternative treatment options. Remember, it may take time and some researching, but there is a treatment option out there to help you or your loved one.

Approach

Different facilities and centers offer different treatment options, and some work better than others. It is for this reason that it is important to do a thorough research on the approach of treatment.

How will you know what works best?

This is where calling out to the different centers will help to see which approach works best for you or the person who needs the treatment.

Some facilities offer a more clinical approach while others are holistic and based on addressing the individuals past traumas. This can seem overwhelming; however, remember that these treatment centers understand and know that. They have had years of experience and can help you make the best choice for yourself or for your family.

Remember...

There is no weakness in asking for help, but more importantly, there is no shame in it as well. When seeking support and guidance for an addiction, the greatest strength comes in taking the first step to getting help.

Nowadays, you can seek help via online chats and messaging, and these options are available to ensure that no one feels left out or that they can't seek help because of access.

If you are in need of assistance or guidance but don't think you can get the help, speak with someone you trust. This can be a friend or family member, and they can help you find the necessary resource. Just with any addiction, remember you are not alone and when you reach out for help, those who care and want what's best for you are going to do what they can to help.

I wish you all the success in the world. You CAN do this!

Resources in Canada

Addiction Centre (https://www.addictioncenter.com/)

The *Addiction Centre* is a one-stop shop that has information for parents, youth, young adults, and support staff. This resource is able to provide in-person resources as well as virtual support. Anyone experiencing a crisis is able to seek support online via their confidential chat rooms or have a counselor call them back.

Available to residents within Canada.

Cedars at Cobble Hill (https://cedarscobblehill.com/)

The *Cedars at Cobble Hill* offers off-site treatment centers that help patients who suffer from a social media addiction. The facility features support staff and trained professionals who help the patients in engaging and overcoming their addiction.

Cedars at Cobble Hill offers medical staff and detox services that help to make the process as painless and smooth as possible.

The center offers around the clock care and medical support. With 13 years and counting of experience, they have helped over 5,000 patients and have a 75% recovery within six-months.

The center also deals with other addictions and are available via telephone or email.

Rideauwood Addiction and Family Services
(https://www.rideauwood.org/)

The *Rideauwood Addiction and Family Services* uses a clinical approach when it comes to managing addictions. They offer services around the clock and with trained and knowledgeable staff. Unlike some treatment centers that focus only on the science, *Rideauwood Addiction and Family Services* looks at adaptive practices that suit the patients' needs.

No treatment is perfect, which is why *Rideauwood Addiction and Family Services* looks at an array of options. Treatment is not a one-size-fits-all approach, which is why they have a four-principle approach to working with their patients.

They offer services around the clock via telephone.

Trafalgar Addiction Treatment Centre
(https://trafalgarresidence.com/)

The *Trafalgar Addiction Treatment Centre* is found in Ontario, Canada, and is considered the best in the region.

Their treatment works with the patients either in-house or as an out-patient. This means that patients have the flexibility and the option of receiving treatment either from the comforts of their home or at one of the clinics.

The center focuses heavily on addressing the mental component of an addiction while also providing patients with the necessary support to overcome an addiction.

Inquiries can be made via telephone, email, or a representative can call back.

Venture Academy (https://www.ventureacademy.ca/)

Venture Academy is a resource that caters mostly to youth and young adults and their social media addiction. The focus is on addressing their addictions and creating long-lasting best practices.

With almost 20 years of service, *Venture Academy* looks to provide unparalleled treatment and services to youth and young adults.

Resources in the USA

American Addiction Centers
(https://americanaddictioncenters.org/)

The American Addiction Centers is an online resource that helps those seeking to find a treatment center. They offer services such as intervention, rehab, and counseling. The American Addiction Center is one of the few US treatment centers that offer their patients a 90-day promise of progress.

What does this mean? It means that the American Addiction Centers is confident in their approach to make a difference and help you with your long-term goals.

The facility understands that it commonly takes 30 days to break a habit when it comes to addiction, but with their 90-day guarantee, they can ensure a proper treatment with lasting power.

Paradigm Treatment (https://paradigmtreatment.com/)

Paradigm Treatment offers in-house treatments for anxiety, depression, trauma, and addiction. The facility specializes in helping teens and young adults.

Their facility is available 24 hours, 7 days a week, to address any questions or for any possible intakes.

With over 10 years servicing the USA and helping those between 12 to 26 years, they understand the impact anxiety, addiction, and depression have on the developing and growing mind.

The facility uses treatment approaches that are best suited to the patient and their disorder. They focus on the patient as an individual and treating the whole person through a mix of traditional, progressive, and evidence-based therapies.

Paradigm Treatment is available to all US residents between 12 to 26 years.

The Ranch Tennessee (https://www.recoveryranch.com)

The Ranch Tennessee understands that all addictions share common roots, and sufferers often have co-occurring disorders. This is why they focus treatment on multiple fronts, utilizing a range of holistic therapies. At the ranch, they take advantage of the beautiful nature that surrounds them. Individuals can even take part in equine therapy, which includes caring for and interacting with the horses at the ranch.

For All Other Resources

Last Door (https://lastdoor.org/)

For resources or a support line, Last Door is a one-stop-website that offers everything from community events to resources on addiction and treatment centers.

Last Door offers 35 years of addiction and rehab services. They run their centers on the principles of compassion, diversity, unity, and integrity.

They offer services both for youth and adult men, as well as a detox facility.

UK Rehab (https://www.uk-rehab.com/)

UK Rehab is a great resource for residents in the United Kingdom. They offer an online chat, telephone, and email service that is available 24 hours, 7 days a week. The website itself offers a lot of information, including an explanation of various treatment therapies.

They are able to direct patients to the necessary resources and services needed when coping with an addiction or mental health problem. At UK Rehab they offer different types of treatments for problems like drugs and alcohol to various behavioral addictions, including internet addiction.

In chapter 8, I mentioned that taking a career assessment test can help you discover your strengths and weaknesses, or to find out what you are passionate about. These kinds of tests are plentiful on the internet. The following are two such resources you can explore.

Good Therapy
(https://www.goodtherapy.org/tests/career-personality-aptitude.html)

Good Therapy offers a comprehensive career personality and aptitude test in both a free and paid version. It is quite comprehensive and consists of 240 questions. Plan on about 45 minutes to complete the online quiz.

Open-Source Psychometrics Project (https://openpsychometrics.org/)

This open source platform has a plethora of personality and psychological quizzes. It exists to assist in research projects and journal articles. It also strives to educate people about the uses of the various quizzes. The anonymized data is only saved if you grant permission.

References

Andersen, C. H. (2015, June 15). *Science Discovers the Real Reason Behind Your Social Media Addiction.* Shape. https://www.shape.com/lifestyle/mind-and-body/scienc e-behind-your-social-media-addiction

Bergland, C. (2013). *The "Love Hormone" Drives Human Urge for Social Connection.* Psychology Today. https://www.psychologytoday.com/us/blog/the-athletes-way/201309/the-love-hormone-drives-human-urge-social -connection

Best Health. (2019, April 14). *5 Happy Hormones And How Boost Them Naturally | Best Health Magazine.* Best Health Magazine Canada. https://www.besthealthmag.ca/best-you/mental-health/h ow-to-boost-your-happy-hormones/

Biomed, A. (2020, May 27). *Serotonin And The Other Happy Hormones In Your Body.* Atlas Biomed Blog | Take Control of Your Health with No-Nonsense News on Lifestyle, Gut Microbes and Genetics. https://atlasbiomed.com/blog/serotonin-and-other-happ y-molecules-made-by-gut-bacteria/

Boateng, W. (2004). Research Alternative for Nursing Practice: A Sociological Perspective. *Gender and Behaviour, 2*(1). https://doi.org/10.4314/gab.v2i1.23318

Chiu, A. (2020, March 4). The TikTok 'skull-breaker challenge' landed a teen in the hospital. Two minors face criminal charges. *Washington Post.* https://www.washingtonpost.com/nation/2020/03/04/t iktok-challenge-skull-breaker/

Cristol, H. (2019, June 19). *What Is Dopamine?* WebMD; WebMD. https://www.webmd.com/mental-health/what-is-dopamine#1

Daily Life. (2019, June 19). *Instant Connection: The Upside to Social Media.* Daily Life. https://dailylife.com/article/the-upside-to-social-media-increased-connection

Deutsch, L. (2020, July 20). Video Games and Grief. Retrieved from https://thegamehers.com/blog/video-games-and-grief

Dfarhud, D., Malmir, M., & Khanahmadi, M. (2014). Happiness & Health: The Biological Factors- Systematic Review Article. *Iranian Journal of Public Health, 43*(11), 1468–1477. https://www.ncbi.nlm.nih.gov/pmc/articles/PMC4449495/

Dimock, M. (2019, January 17). *Defining generations: Where Millennials End and Generation Z Begins.* Pew Research Center. https://www.pewresearch.org/fact-tank/2019/01/17/where-millennials-end-and-generation-z-begins/

Eisenberger, N. I., & Lieberman, M. D. (2005). Why It Hurts to Be Left Out: THe Neurocognitive Overlap Between Physical and Social Pain. *The Social Outcst: Ostracism, Social Exclusion, Rejection, and Bullying, 109*(130).

Falk, E. B., Berkman, E. T., & Lieberman, M. D. (2012). From Neural Responses to Population Behavior. *Psychological Science, 23*(5), 439–445. https://doi.org/10.1177/0956797611434964

Games for grieving - how video games can help with bereavement. (n.d.). Marie Curie. Retrieved January 15, 2021, from https://www.mariecurie.org.uk/blog/video-games-to-help-with-grief/278671

Gillis, M. E. (2019, September 19). *Cyberbullying on rise in US: 12-year-old was "all-American little girl" before suicide.* Fox News; Fox News. https://www.foxnews.com/health/cyberbullying-all-amer ican-little-girl-suicide

Haynes, T. (2018, April 30). *Science in the News.* Science in the News. http://sitn.hms.harvard.edu/flash/2018/dopamine-smart phones-battle-time/

Heath, S. (Ed.). (2016, August 25). *How Social Media Support Groups Enhance Patient Experience.* PatientEngagementHIT. https://patientengagementhit.com/news/how-social-me dia-support-groups-enhance-patient-experience

Hyatt, M. (2015, July 17). *It's Not all Bad News: The Upside of Social Media.* Michael Hyatt. https://michaelhyatt.com/upside-of-social-media/

Kitterman, T. (2018, September 20). Infographic: The science behind social media addiction - PR Daily. *PR Daily.* https://www.prdaily.com/infographic-the-science-behind -social-media-addiction/

Leiner, B. M., Cerf, V. G., & Clark, D. D. (2017). *Brief History of the Internet | Internet Society.* Internet Society. https://www.internetsociety.org/internet/history-internet /brief-history-internet/

Lieberman, M. D. (2007). Social Cognitive Neuroscience: A Review of Core Processes. *Annual Review of Psychology, 58*(1), 259–289. https://doi.org/10.1146/annurev.psych.58.110405.08565 4

McSweeney, K. (2019). *This is Your Brain on Instagram: Effects of Social Media on the Brain.* Northrop Grumman. https://now.northropgrumman.com/this-is-your-brain-o n-instagram-effects-of-social-media-on-the-brain/

Monroy, L. (2019, March 18). *Can Making the Bed in the Morning Make You Happier?* Best Mattress Brand. https://bestmattress-brand.org/making-the-bed/

National Institution on Mental Health. (2018, May 10). *NIMH » Suicide.* Nih.Gov. https://www.nimh.nih.gov/health/statistics/suicide.shtml

Pantic, I. (2014). Online Social Networking and Mental Health. *Cyberpsychology, Behavior, and Social Networking, 17*(10), 652–657. https://doi.org/10.1089/cyber.2014.0070

Penenberg, A. L. (2010, July 1). *Social Networking Affects Brains Like Falling in Love.* Fast Company. https://www.fastcompany.com/1659062/social-networking-affects-brains-falling-love

Ra, C. K., Cho, J., Stone, M. D., De La Cerda, J., Goldenson, N. I., Moroney, E., Tung, I., Lee, S. S., & Leventhal, A. M. (2018). Association of Digital Media Use With Subsequent Symptoms of Attention-Deficit/Hyperactivity Disorder Among Adolescents. *JAMA, 320*(3), 255. https://doi.org/10.1001/jama.2018.8931

Robinson, L., & Smith, M. (2020, January 16). *Social Media and Mental Health - HelpGuide.org.* Https://Www.Helpguide.org. https://www.helpguide.org/articles/mental-health/social-media-and-mental-health.htm

Rudin, A. (2010, June 28). *The Science Behind Feeling Good While Social Networking.* HuffPost. https://www.huffpost.com/entry/the-science-behind-feelin_b_624649#:~:text=Created%20with%20Sketch.-

Sigala, M. (2018, January 2). *The Hidden Costs Of Selfie Tourism.* Bodyandsoulau. https://www.bodyandsoul.com.au/mind-body/travel/the-hidden-costs-of-selfie-tourism/news-story/e80b3d8254e2216713617fa04e65c0c3

Skelly, M. (2012). Physiology 2012: The undergraduate experience. *Physiology News, 7*(Autumn 2012), 12–12. https://doi.org/10.36866/pn.88.12

Smart Social. (2018, October 17). *10 Examples on the Positive Impact of Social Media.* Smart Social. https://smartsocial.com/positive-impact-of-social-media/

Tiffany, K. (2019, December 23). *Why Kids Online Are Chasing 'Clout.'* The Atlantic. https://www.theatlantic.com/technology/archive/2019/12/clout-definition-meme-influencers-social-capital-youtube/603895/

Wallner, L., & Kirch, M. A. (2016). Online Social Engagement by Cancer Patients: A Clinic-Based Patient Survey. *JMIR Cancer, 2*(2), e10. https://doi.org/10.2196/cancer.5785

Ward, B., Ward, M., Fried, O., & Paskhover, B. (2018). Nasal Distortion in Short-Distance Photographs: The Selfie Effect. *JAMA Facial Plastic Surgery, 20*(4), 333. https://doi.org/10.1001/jamafacial.2018.0009

Webwise. (2014, June 10). *Explained: What is Twitter? -.* Webwise.Ie. https://www.webwise.ie/parents/explained-what-is-twitter-2/

What is Twitter and why should you use it? - Economic and Social Research Council. (2018). Ukri.org; ESRC. https://esrc.ukri.org/research/impact-toolkit/social-media/twitter/what-is-twitter/

Wikipedia. (2020, January 16). *Catfish: The TV Show*. Wikipedia;
    Wikimedia   Foundation.
    https://en.wikipedia.org/wiki/Catfish:_The_TV_Show

Wojcik, S., & Hughes, A. (2019, April 24). *Sizing Up Twitter Users*.
    Pew Research Center: Internet, Science & Tech; Pew
    Research   Center: Internet,   Science   &   Tech.
    https://www.pewresearch.org/internet/2019/04/24/sizi
    ng-up-twitter-users/